APPALACHIAN TRAIL

Data Book

2014

APPALACHIAN TRAIL

Data Book

2014

THIRTY-SIXTH EDITION

Daniel D. Chazin, *Editor*

APPALACHIAN TRAIL
CONSERVANCY

Harpers Ferry

Thirty-sixth edition
First published in 1977

ISBN 978-1-889386-85-0

MIX
Paper from
responsible sources
FSC® C010897

Contents

Notice to All Trail Users

The information in this publication is the result of the best effort of the publisher, using data available to it at the time of printing. Changes resulting from maintenance work and relocations are constantly occurring and, therefore, no published route can be regarded as precisely accurate at the time you read this notice.

Notices of pending relocations are indicated in current Appalachian Trail guidebooks, whenever possible.

Because maintenance of the Trail is conducted by volunteers and maintaining clubs listed in the appropriate guidebooks, questions about the exact route of the Trail should be addressed to the maintaining clubs or the Appalachian Trail Conservancy, P.O. Box 807, Harpers Ferry, WV 25425 (telephone: 304-535-6331; e-mail: <info@appalachiantrail.org>). On the Trail, please pay close attention to — and follow — the white blazes and any directional signs.

There are few things more rewarding than hiking the Appalachian Trail, whether you come to it as a novice looking to spend only a couple of hours outdoors or a Trail-tested veteran who has thru-hiked more than once.

Regardless of your skill, it is extremely important to plan your hike, especially in places where water is scarce. Purify water drawn from any source. Water purity cannot be guaranteed. The Appalachian Trail Conservancy and the various maintaining clubs attempt to locate good sources of water along the Trail but have no control over those sources and cannot, in any sense, be responsible for the quality of the water at any given time. You should ensure the safety of all water you use by treating it.

Certain risks are inherent in any Appalachian Trail hike. Each A.T. user must accept personal responsibility for his or her safety while on the Trail. The Appalachian Trail Conservancy and its member maintaining clubs cannot ensure the safety of any hiker on the Trail, and, when undertaking a hike on the Trail, each user thereby assumes the risk for any accident, illness, or injury that might occur on the Trail.

Enjoy your hike, but please take all appropriate precautions for your safety and well-being.

Safety and Ethics

Although the Appalachian Trail is safer than most places, you should be aware that problems do occur, and a few crimes of violence have occurred during the past three decades. Safety awareness is one of your best lines of defense. Be aware of what you are doing, where you are, and to whom you are talking. Here are some suggestions:

- *Use extra caution if hiking alone.* If you are by yourself and encounter a stranger who makes you feel uncomfortable, say you are with a group that is behind you. Be creative. If in doubt, move on.

- *Leave your hiking itinerary and timetable* with someone at home. Be sure he or she knows your Trail name, if you have one. Check in regularly, and establish a procedure to follow if you fail to check in. It helps to let ATC know your name and Trail name, in case a family member needs to reach you during an extended hike. However, *do not broadcast your itinerary or location in real time* on on-line journals or blogs.

- *Be wary of strangers.* Be friendly, but cautious. Don't tell strangers your plans. Avoid people who act suspiciously, hostile, or intoxicated.

- *Don't camp near road crossings.*

- *Dress conservatively* to avoid unwanted attention. You, too, guys!

- *Carrying firearms is strongly discouraged.* Although now legal to carry (but not discharge) on National Park Service lands and in most other areas, with the proper state-by-state permits, they could be turned against you, you face a high risk of an accidental shooting, and they are extra weight.

- *Eliminate opportunities for theft.* Don't bring jewelry. Hide your money. If you must leave your pack, hide it carefully, or leave it with someone trustworthy. Don't leave valuables or equipment (especially in sight) in vehicles parked at Trailheads.

- *Use the Trail and shelter registers.* Sign in, leave a note, and report any suspicious activities. If someone needs to locate you, or if a serious crime has been committed along the Trail, the first place authorities will look is in the registers.

- *Report any crime or harassment* to the local law-enforcement authorities *and* ATC. Send an e-mail to <incident@appalachiantrail.org> or call (304) 535-6331.

As the A.T. becomes increasingly used, the potential for problems could increase. Help to keep the Trail a safe place. Maintain your safety awareness, help each other, and report all incidents. *More detailed advice is available at <www.appalachiantrail.org/safetyawareness>.* Be prudent and cautious without allowing common sense to slip into paranoia. Trust your gut.

Reporting Trail Emergencies

Check the map, guidebook, nearest shelter, or Trailhead facility for local emergency telephone numbers. Leave the Trail at the nearest road crossing, and find a telephone or cellular-phone reception. Know your location and the location of the incident as precisely as possible. Dial "911" or "0" (ask the operator to connect you with the nearest state-police facility), and make your report. Ask the officer to notify the Appalachian Trail Conservancy at (304) 535-6331.

Public Transportation and Shuttles

The Appalachian Trail Conservancy maintains information on public transportation to the Trail and available shuttle providers on its Web site at <www.appalachiantrail.org/shuttles>.

Leave No Trace

The Appalachian Trail Conservancy, in partnership with Leave No Trace, Inc., asks you to help take care of the Appalachian Trail and the wild country it passes through. Please do your part by following the seven Leave No Trace principles of low-impact use while in the backcountry:

1. Plan ahead and prepare.
2. Travel and camp on durable surfaces.
3. Dispose of waste properly.
4. Leave what you find.
5. Minimize campfire impacts.
6. Respect wildlife.
7. Be considerate of other visitors.

More specific ways those principles apply to the Appalachian Trail can be found at <www.appalachiantrail.org/Lnt>. The continued existence of the Trail depends, in part, on proper use by those who walk on it. Particular care should be taken not to damage the footpath itself, natural features alongside it, or the property of others, through littering or other vandalism, improper fires, or use of vehicles. The needs of other users should always be considered, and special regulations must be followed in many areas. Please keep day-hiking groups to 25 people or fewer and overnight groups to no more than 10 people.

Although more than 99 percent of the Appalachian Trail now crosses public land, the remainder is on private property, thanks to the cooperation and good faith of the landowners. The Conservancy and its member clubs strongly urge all users of the Trail to respect those private lands and the owners' rights as if the lands were their own.

Public lands are, in a sense, the user's own—shared with all other users—so please proceed accordingly, taking care to obey any regulations imposed on use of the Trail in a particular section. **For example, camping permits are required before entering Great Smoky Mountains National Park.** On many other parts of the Trail, camping is permitted only in designated areas.

Again, please consult the guidebooks and maps, and watch for special signs along the Trail.

And, enjoy your hike!

Useful Features of the *A.T. Data Book*

This publication provides a ready reference for hikers to the major features of the Appalachian Trail as it winds for more than 2,185 miles from Maine to Georgia. Many hikers find it indispensable to their journeys on the A.T. and save each year's edition with a record of their experiences and accomplishments.

The features listed here include shelters and campsites, road crossings, sources of water, elevations, principal mountain peaks and gaps, and other notable physical landmarks of America's foremost national scenic trail. Locations of areas where lodging, meals, groceries, and post offices are available also are listed, with distances and directions. Additionally, each section is marked with the Trail-maintaining club associated with that segment, and Web-site information for the clubs may be found on page 85.

The *Data Book* is intended to be useful in broad-scale planning of a trip of any length on the Trail, from home or while on the footpath itself.

The *Data Book* does not, however, include sufficient detail for careful, complete planning of a trip. Potential hikers are encouraged to purchase separately the official *Appalachian Trail Guide* bok-and-maps set for the state(s) they plan to hike. The guidebooks contain detailed descriptions of Trail sections, facilities near the Trail, points of interest off the Trail, background on the history and natural features of the area, and other important information.

All guidebooks are sold with sets of maps for the state(s) described, another key to a safe and enjoyable hike. Guidebooks, maps, and other ATC publications may be ordered by visiting the Ultimate A.T. Store *via* <www.appalachiantrail.org>. Or, call (304) 728-5143 or toll-free at (888) 287-8673 (AT STORE). Membership in the Appalachian Trail Conservancy carries with it a discount on guidebooks and other publications.

The compilation of each edition of the *Data Book* begins with the latest *Appalachian Trail Guides*. The distances and descriptive information are updated to take into account relocations since the last edition.

This information is supplied to the Conservancy by its member clubs and volunteers who help ensure access to the Appalachian Trail experience for all. Each year more than 6,000 volunteers contribute more than 200,000 hours of work to various projects along the Trail.

The data has been cross-checked by both volunteers and staff members. However, it is impossible to ensure absolute accuracy of the information, and changes may occur during the year of this edition. Trail-enhancing relocations that affect distances between major features are underway in some states. Also, severe weather conditions, fires, and other unpredictable developments might force temporary closings of a section.

Users of the Trail for any period of time should carefully follow the painted white blazes that mark the current route of the Trail.

Hikers finding errors or omissions in the *Data Book* are urged to report them, by e-mail to <publisher@appalachiantrail.org>, or by mail to Data Book Editor, Appalachian Trail Conservancy, P.O. Box 807, Harpers Ferry, WV 25425. Confirmed changes will be included in the next edition.

How to Use the *Data Book*

The *Data Book* is divided into twelve chapters, beginning with Maine (at Katahdin) and ending with the Approach Trail to Springer Mountain in Georgia. With one exception, each chapter corresponds to a volume in the current series of *Appalachian Trail Guides* (see page 4 for ordering information). The section beginning on page 27, for example, matches the third volume in the guidebook series, which covers the Trail in Massachusetts–Connecticut. The exception is the Trail route through the Great Smokies of Tennessee and North Carolina, which is covered in both the Tennessee–North Carolina and North Carolina–Georgia guidebooks. It is included here only in Chapter Ten (Tennessee–North Carolina).

Trail-maintaining clubs are listed in the outside margins next to the section(s) of Trail that each club maintains. The beginning and ending points of each club's range are indicated by a small gray rectangle. Web site information for the clubs may be found on page 85.

Georgia A.T. Club

Trail sections, as numbered and identified in the corresponding guide, are given in the columns to the left on each page, under the heading *GBS* (guidebook section). Sections are numbered consecutively, from north to south, within each state.

N.C. Section 11

In the right column, under the heading *Map*, the number of the map that covers the area is given. For more detail about a particular feature or section of the Trail, consult the relevant guidebook section or map.

Each section contains a list of features along or near the Trail.

Towns with post offices (P.O.) are printed in boldface and carry their ZIP Code in the listing. Towns without post offices are listed only if the Trail goes directly through them; "P.O." is omitted in those cases.

Greenwood Lake, N.Y., P.O. 10925

The *elevations* of selected points along the Trail follow the name of the feature. Those elevations are intended to represent the most significant points in terms of elevation gain and loss and provide the hiker with a general sense of the elevation change along each section of the hike. Of course, many ups and downs have not been referenced in this book, and the difficulty of the terrain may vary considerably. Hikers should use the elevations provided only as a general guide.

Rainbow Ledges (1,517')

In general, all *facilities* within five miles of the Trail by road are included, unless similar facilities are located closer to the footpath or a facility's inclusion would not significantly benefit the hiker. In some cases, where a particular facility is not available for a great distance, we have included facilities that are more than five miles from the Trail but still within 12 miles.

To the right of the list of features, facilities, if any, are noted with a one-letter code. The codes are explained on pages 8–9.

Low Gap   Cw

Except for shelters, campsites, and water sources located on the Trail itself—or within 0.1 mile of the footpath—the listing for a facility includes the distance and direction to it. So, if the symbols "C", "S", or "w" appear without direction and distance information in the listing, that campsite, shelter, or water source is on the Trail or within about 500 feet of it.

The number to the left of a feature is the *distance* — in miles — of the feature from the northern end of the part of the Trail covered in that particular chapter (read down). The number to the right of the features and facilities lists, correspondingly, is the feature's distance from the southern end of the part of the Trail covered by this chapter (read up). The starting point for the cumulative distance is given at the top of the column.

Miles from Katahdin		Miles from Maine–N.H. Line
0.0	Katahdin (Baxter Peak) (5,268')	281.4
1.0	Thoreau Spring	w 280.4

Sometimes the Trail follows a road, ridge line, lake, creek, or other physical feature for some distance. In those cases, usually only one distance is listed. For roads, this is generally the point at which the Trail first reaches the road proceeding from north to south, or, in some cases, the point representing the end of the section. For ridge lines, this is the highest point. Again, for more complete information about a particular feature, please consult the guidebooks, maps, or both.

Abbreviations

C — *Campsites and campgrounds.* Unless otherwise indicated, water is available. For New Hampshire, the "C" code is also used to indicate those shelters at which tent camping also is permitted.

E — *"East,"* used to designate direction to facilities that are to the right of the Trail when traveling north (*i.e.,* toward Katahdin).

G — *Groceries, supplies.*

L   *Lodgings other than Trail shelters, campsites, and campgrounds:* for example, motels, hotels, cottages, and hostels. This code is also used for the Appalachian Mountain Club (AMC) huts in New Hampshire and camps (commercial cottages) in Maine.

m   *Miles.*

M   *Meals; restaurants.*

nw   *No potable water.* This is used in shelter and campsite listings only.

P.O.   *Post office.* Towns without post offices are listed only if the Trail goes directly through them; "P.O." is omitted in those cases.

R   *Road access.* Only roads open to the public and passable by ordinary automobiles are designated. Included are road crossings and locations where the Trail runs along a road or is adjacent to a road that provides access to the Trail. Where the road crossings are frequent (every two miles or less), lesser ones are omitted.

S   *Shelter.* A three-sided structure, with or without bunks or floors, intended as overnight housing for hikers (also known as lean-tos in some areas). Included in this category are unlocked cabins or lodges, found primarily in New Hampshire, Vermont, Pennsylvania, and Maryland. (See also "L".)

W   *"West,"* used to designate direction to facilities that are to the left of the Trail when traveling north (*i.e.,* toward Katahdin).

w   *Water* (from springs, streams, *etc.*). In general, where available, water sources are listed about every three to four miles. Other water sources do exist, and not every water source is listed in the *Data Book*. **Note: All water should be purified before use.**

☆   Indicates an **Appalachian Trail Community**, a town designated by the ATC as a participant in A.T. protection work through local education initiatives and land-conservation activity, for example, while ATC helps it with "green tourism" development. A list of designated towns and counties can be found on page 87.

Appalachian Trail Distances

These sections and Trail points correspond to the beginnings and endings of chapters in this book and the eleven-volume series of official Appalachian Trail Guides.

Length by Section

Maine	281.8
New Hampshire–Vermont	310.7
Massachusetts–Connecticut	141.1
New York–New Jersey	161.9
Pennsylvania	229.3
Maryland–West Virginia–Northern Virginia	94.9
Shenandoah National Park	107.8
Central Virginia	226.0
Southwest Virginia	164.4
Tennessee–North Carolina	300.9
North Carolina–Georgia	166.5

Cumulative Distances

Miles from Katahdin		Miles from Springer Mountain
0.0	Baxter Peak, Katahdin, Maine	2,185.3
281.8	Maine–New Hampshire Line	1,903.5
592.5	Vermont–Massachusetts Line	1,592.8
733.6	Connecticut–New York Line	1,451.7
895.5	New Jersey–Pennsylvania Line	1,289.8
1,124.8	Pennsylvania–Maryland Line	1,060.5
1,219.7	Front Royal, Virginia	965.6
1,327.5	Rockfish Gap, Virginia	857.8
1,553.5	New River, Virginia	631.8
1,717.9	Damascus, Virginia	467.4
2,018.8	Fontana Dam, North Carolina	166.5
2,185.3	Springer Mountain, Georgia	0.0

GBS	N to S	Features	Facilities (see page 8 for codes)	S to N	Map

Miles from Katahdin

Miles from Maine–N.H. Line

	N to S	Features	Facilities	S to N	
	0.0	Katahdin (Baxter Peak) (5,268')		281.8	
	1.0	Thoreau Spring	w	280.8	
	4.0	Katahdin Stream Falls	w	277.8	
	5.2	Katahdin Stream Campground, Birches Campsite (1,070') (C,S,w on A.T.)	CSw	276.6	
	5.3	Cross Tote Road	R	276.5	
	7.5	Daicey Pond Campground Road (L,w 0.1m E)	RLw	274.3	
	8.8	Big Niagara Falls	w	273.0	
	9.6	Upper Fork Nesowadnehunk Stream (ford)	w	272.2	
	10.5	Lower Fork Nesowadnehunk Stream (ford)	w	271.3	
	11.0	Pine Point	w	270.8	
	14.0	Katahdin Stream	w	267.8	
	14.4	Abol Stream, Baxter Park Boundary		267.4	
	15.1	Abol Bridge over West Branch of Penobscot River; junction with International A.T. (588') (C,G,w on A.T.)	RCGw	266.7	
	18.6	Hurd Brook Lean-to (710')	Sw	263.2	
	21.1	Rainbow Ledges (1,517')		260.7	
	22.9	Rainbow Lake (east end)	w	258.9	
	26.3	Rainbow Spring Campsite	Cw	255.5	
	28.1	Rainbow Lake (west end) Side Trail	w	253.7	
	30.1	Rainbow Stream Lean-to (1,020')	Sw	251.7	
	32.5	Pollywog Stream (682')	w	249.3	
	33.9	Crescent Pond (west end)	w	247.9	
	36.3	Nesuntabunt Mountain (1,520')		245.5	
	38.2	Wadleigh Stream Lean-to	Sw	243.6	
	40.8	Nahmakanta Lake (south end) (650')	Rw	241.0	

Maine Section 1

Maine Section 2

Maine A.T. Club

Maine Map 1

Maine

	Miles from Katahdin			*Miles from Maine–N.H. Line*	
	42.5	Tumbledown Dick Trail		239.3	
	44.0	Nahmakanta Stream Campsite	Cw	237.8	
	46.0	Logging Road	R		
		(C,L,M 1m E)	RCLM	235.8	
	47.7	Pemadumcook Lake (southwest shore)	w	234.1	
	48.3	Potaywadjo Spring Lean-to (710')	Sw	233.5	
	50.1	Sand Beach, Lower Jo-Mary Lake	w	231.7	
	51.8	Antlers Campsite (500')	Cw	230.0	
	53.1	Mud Pond (outlet)	w	228.7	
	56.0	Jo-Mary Road			
		(w on A.T.; C,G 6m E)	RCGw	225.8	
	59.7	Cooper Brook Falls Lean-to (880')	Sw	222.1	
	62.0	Crawford Pond (outlet)	w	219.8	
	62.9	Kokadjo–B Pond Road	R	218.9	
	64.3	Little Boardman Mountain (1,980')		217.5	
	65.6	Spring	w	216.2	
	65.9	Mountain View Pond (outlet)	w	215.9	
	67.5	East Branch of Pleasant River (ford)	w	214.3	
	67.8	East Branch Lean-to (1,225')	Sw	214.0	
	69.8	West Branch Ponds Road			
		(L,M 4m W)	RLM	212.0	
	71.4	Logan Brook Lean-to (2,480')	Sw	210.4	
	72.8	White Cap Mountain (3,650')		209.0	
	73.9	White Brook Trail		207.9	
	74.5	Hay Mountain		207.3	
	76.1	West Peak		205.7	
	76.8	Sidney Tappan Campsite (2,425')	Cw	205.0	
	77.7	Gulf Hagas Mountain		204.1	
	78.6	Carl A. Newhall Lean-to (1,860')	Sw	203.2	
	82.1	Gulf Hagas Cut-off Trail	w	199.7	

Maine A.T. Club — *Maine Section 3* — *Maine Map 2*

Maine

Miles from Katahdin

Miles from Maine–N.H. Line

	N to S	Features	Facilities	S to N	
Maine 3	82.8	Gulf Hagas Trail	w	199.0	Map 2
	83.8	The Hermitage (695')			
		(C,w 0.7m E)	Cw	198.0	
	84.1	West Branch of Pleasant River (ford)	w	197.7	
	84.6	Katahdin Iron Works Road	R	197.2	
	85.8	East Chairback Pond Side Trail (1,630')			
		(w 0.2m W)	w	196.0	
	88.0	Chairback Mountain (2,180')		193.8	
	88.5	Chairback Gap Lean-to (1,930')	Sw	193.3	
	88.9	Columbus Mountain (2,325')		192.9	
	90.2	West Chairback Pond Side Trail (1,770')	w	191.6	
	90.8	Third Mountain, Monument Cliff (1,920')		191.0	
	93.3	Fourth Mountain (2,380')		188.5	
Maine Section 4	95.4	Cloud Pond Lean-to Side Trail			Maine Map 3
		(S,w 0.3m E)	Sw	186.4	
	96.3	Barren Mountain (2,660')		185.5	
	99.4	Long Pond Stream Lean-to (940')	Sw	182.4	
	100.2	Long Pond Stream (ford) (620')	w	181.6	
	104.1	Wilson Valley Lean-to (1,045')	Sw	177.7	
	104.5	Montreal, Maine & Atlantic Railroad		177.3	
	104.8	Big Wilson Stream (ford) (600')	w	177.0	
	107.7	Little Wilson Stream	w	174.1	
	107.9	Little Wilson Falls		173.9	
	110.7	North Pond (outlet)	w	171.1	
	111.5	Leeman Brook Lean-to (1,060')	Sw	170.3	
	112.6	Lily Pond	w	169.2	
	113.3	Bell Pond	w	168.5	
	114.4	Spectacle Pond (outlet)	w	167.4	
	114.5	Maine 15 (1,215')	R	167.3	

Maine A.T. Club

Maine

Miles from Katahdin

Miles from Maine–N.H. Line

	N to S	Features	Facilities	S to N	
	117.8	**Monson, Maine, P.O. 04464** (900')	☆		
		(P.O.,C,G,L,M 2m E)	CGLM	164.0	
	120.8	Shirley–Blanchard Road	R	161.0	
	121.2	East Branch of Piscataquis River (ford)	w	160.6	
	123.5	Horseshoe Canyon Lean-to (870')	Sw	158.3	
	126.6	West Branch of Piscataquis River (ford)	w	155.2	
	130.3	Bald Mountain Pond (outlet)	w	151.5	
	132.4	Moxie Bald Lean-to (1,220')	Sw	149.4	
	134.5	Moxie Bald Mountain (2,629')		147.3	
	136.5	Bald Mountain Brook Lean-to (1,300')	Sw	145.3	
	139.3	Moxie Pond (south end) (970')	Rw	142.5	
	144.2	Pleasant Pond Mountain (2,470')		137.6	
	145.5	Pleasant Pond Lean-to (1,320')	Sw	136.3	
	145.9	Boise-Cascade Logging Road	R	135.9	
	148.5	Holly Brook	w	133.3	
	151.2	U.S. 201; **Caratunk, Maine, P.O. 04925**			
		(P.O. 0.3m E; C,L,M 2.0m W)	RCLM	130.6	
	151.5	Kennebec River (490')	w	130.3	
	154.8	Trail to Harrison's Pierce Pond Camps			
		(L,M 0.3m E; w 0.1m E)	RLMw	127.0	
	155.2	Pierce Pond Lean-to (1,160')	Sw	126.6	
	158.7	North Branch of Carrying Place Stream	w	123.1	
	159.4	Logging Road	R	122.4	
	161.1	East Carry Pond (north end)	w	120.7	
	162.6	Sandy Stream, Middle Carry Pond (inlet)	w	119.2	
	164.5	West Carry Pond (east side)	w	117.3	
	165.2	West Carry Pond Lean-to (1,340')	Sw	116.6	
	165.9	West Carry Pond (west side)	w	115.9	
	167.0	Roundtop Mountain (1,760')		114.8	
	168.7	Long Falls Dam Road (1,225')	R	113.1	

Maine A.T. Club — Maine Section 5 — Maine Section 6

Maine Map 4 — Maine Map 5

Maine

Miles from Katahdin

Miles from Maine–N.H. Line

	N to S	Features	Facilities	S to N	
	170.4	Campsite	Cw	111.4	
	171.4	Bog Brook Road, Flagstaff Lake (inlet)	Rw	110.4	
	171.5	East Flagstaff Road	R	110.3	
	172.9	Little Bigelow Lean-to (1,760')	Sw	108.9	
	174.6	Little Bigelow Mountain (east end) (3,010')		107.2	
	177.8	Safford Notch Campsite (2,230') (C,w 0.3m E)	Cw	104.0	
	177.9	Safford Brook Trail		103.9	
	179.8	Bigelow Mountain (Avery Peak) (4,090')		102.0	
	180.2	Avery Memorial Campsite, Bigelow Col, Fire Warden's Trail	Cw	101.6	
	180.5	Bigelow Mountain (West Peak) (4,145')		101.3	
	182.6	South Horn		99.2	
	183.1	Horns Pond Lean-tos (3,160')	CSw	98.7	
	183.3	Horns Pond Trail		98.5	
	185.0	Bigelow Range Trail, Cranberry Pond (w 0.2m W)	w	96.8	
	186.3	Cranberry Stream Campsite (1,350')	Cw	95.5	
	187.2	Stratton Brook (1,230')	w	94.6	
	187.4	Stratton Brook Pond Road	R	94.4	
	188.2	Maine 27; **Stratton, Maine, P.O. 04982** (P.O.,G,L,M 5m W)	RGLM	93.6	
	193.4	North Crocker Mountain (4,228')		88.4	
	194.4	South Crocker Mountain (4,040')		87.4	
	195.5	Crocker Cirque Campsite Side Trail (2,710') (w on A.T.; C 0.2m E)	Cw	86.3	
	196.5	Caribou Valley Road (2,220')		85.3	
	196.6	South Branch Carrabassett River (ford)	w	85.2	
	198.8	Sugarloaf Mountain Trail		83.0	
	200.9	Spaulding Mountain (4,000')		80.9	

Maine Section 7

Maine Section 8

Maine Map 5

Maine Map 6

Maine A.T. Club

Maine

GBS	N to S	Features	Facilities (see page 8 for codes)	S to N	Map

Miles from Katahdin

Miles from Maine–N.H. Line

<table>
<tr><td></td><td>201.7</td><td>Spaulding Mountain Lean-to (3,140')</td><td>Sw</td><td>80.1</td><td></td></tr>
<tr><td></td><td>202.8</td><td>Mt. Abraham Trail</td><td></td><td>79.0</td><td></td></tr>
<tr><td></td><td>203.9</td><td>Lone Mountain (3,260')</td><td></td><td>77.9</td><td></td></tr>
<tr><td></td><td>207.0</td><td>Orbeton Stream (ford) (1,550')</td><td>w</td><td>74.8</td><td></td></tr>
<tr><td></td><td>209.7</td><td>Poplar Ridge Lean-to (2,960')</td><td>Sw</td><td>72.1</td><td></td></tr>
<tr><td></td><td>210.7</td><td>Stream</td><td>w</td><td>71.1</td><td></td></tr>
<tr><td></td><td>211.1</td><td>Saddleback Junior (3,655')</td><td></td><td>70.7</td><td></td></tr>
<tr><td></td><td>212.4</td><td>Redington Stream Campsite</td><td>Cw</td><td>69.4</td><td></td></tr>
<tr><td></td><td>213.1</td><td>The Horn (4,040')</td><td></td><td>68.7</td><td></td></tr>
<tr><td></td><td>214.7</td><td>Saddleback Mountain (4,120')</td><td></td><td>67.1</td><td></td></tr>
<tr><td></td><td>216.7</td><td>Eddy Pond</td><td>w</td><td>65.1</td><td></td></tr>
<tr><td></td><td>218.6</td><td>Piazza Rock Lean-to (2,065')</td><td>Sw</td><td>63.2</td><td></td></tr>
<tr><td></td><td>220.3</td><td>Sandy River (1,595')</td><td>w</td><td>61.5</td><td></td></tr>
<tr><td></td><td>220.4</td><td>Maine 4; Rangeley, Maine, P.O. 04970</td><td>☆</td><td></td><td></td></tr>
<tr><td></td><td></td><td>(P.O.,C,G,L,M 9m W)</td><td>RCGLM</td><td>61.4</td><td></td></tr>
<tr><td></td><td>222.5</td><td>South Pond (2,174')</td><td>w</td><td>59.3</td><td></td></tr>
<tr><td></td><td>225.2</td><td>Little Swift River Pond Campsite (2,460')</td><td>Cw</td><td>56.6</td><td></td></tr>
<tr><td></td><td>229.8</td><td>Sabbath Day Pond Lean-to</td><td>Sw</td><td>52.0</td><td></td></tr>
<tr><td></td><td>230.1</td><td>Long Pond (2,330')</td><td>w</td><td>51.7</td><td></td></tr>
<tr><td></td><td>231.9</td><td>Moxie Pond</td><td>w</td><td>49.9</td><td></td></tr>
<tr><td></td><td>233.5</td><td>Maine 17; Oquossoc, Maine, P.O. 04964</td><td></td><td></td><td></td></tr>
<tr><td></td><td></td><td>(P.O.,G,L,M 11m W)</td><td>RGLM</td><td>48.3</td><td></td></tr>
<tr><td></td><td>234.3</td><td>Bemis Stream (ford) (1,495')</td><td>w</td><td>47.5</td><td></td></tr>
<tr><td></td><td>238.1</td><td>Bemis Mountain Lean-to (2,800')</td><td>Sw</td><td>43.7</td><td></td></tr>
<tr><td></td><td>239.8</td><td>Bemis Range (West Peak) (3,580')</td><td></td><td>42.0</td><td></td></tr>
<tr><td></td><td>240.8</td><td>Bemis Stream Trail</td><td></td><td>41.0</td><td></td></tr>
<tr><td></td><td>244.0</td><td>Old Blue Mountain (3,600')</td><td></td><td>37.8</td><td></td></tr>
<tr><td></td><td>246.8</td><td>South Arm Road, Black Brook (ford) (1,410')</td><td></td><td></td><td></td></tr>
<tr><td></td><td></td><td>(w on A.T.; C,G 4.5m W)</td><td>RCGw</td><td>35.0</td><td></td></tr>
<tr><td></td><td>248.6</td><td>Moody Mountain (2,440)</td><td></td><td>33.2</td><td></td></tr>
</table>

Left margin: Maine A.T. Club — Maine Section 8 — Maine Section 9 — Maine 10 — Maine 11

Right margin: Maine Map 6 — Maine Map 7

Maine

	N to S	Features	Facilities	S to N	
	Miles from Katahdin		*Miles from Maine–N.H. Line*		
	249.5	Sawyer Notch, Sawyer Brook (ford) (1,095')	w	32.3	
	250.9	Hall Mountain Lean-to (2,650')	Sw	30.9	
	252.2	Wyman Mountain (2,920')		29.6	
	255.1	Surplus Pond (outlet)	w	26.7	
	256.9	East B Hill Road (1,485'); **Andover, Maine, P.O. 04216** (P.O.,C,G,L,M 8m E)	RCGLM	24.9	
	257.7	Dunn Notch and Falls	w	24.1	
	261.4	Frye Notch Lean-to (2,280')	Sw	20.4	
	263.2	Baldpate Mountain (East Peak), Grafton Loop Trail (3,810')		18.6	
	264.1	Baldpate Mountain (West Peak) (3,662')		17.7	
	264.9	Baldpate Lean-to (2,660')	Sw	16.9	
	267.2	Grafton Notch, Maine 26 (1,495')	R	14.6	
	268.3	Brook	w	13.5	
	270.7	Old Speck Trail, Grafton Loop Trail (3,985')		11.1	
	271.8	Speck Pond Campsite, Speck Pond Trail	CSw	10.0	
	272.7	Mahoosuc Arm (3,770')		9.1	
	274.3	Mahoosuc Notch (east end) (2,150')	w	7.5	
	275.4	Mahoosuc Notch (west end), Mahoosuc Notch Trail	w	6.4	
	276.4	Fulling Mill Mountain (South Peak) (3,395')		5.4	
	276.9	Full Goose Shelter and Campsite	CSw	4.9	
	277.9	Goose Eye Mountain (North Peak)		3.9	
	279.1	Goose Eye Mountain (East Peak) (3,790')		2.7	
	280.9	Mt. Carlo (3,565')		0.9	
	281.3	Carlo Col Trail, Carlo Col Shelter and Campsite (C,S,w 0.3m W)	CSw	0.5	
	281.8	Maine–New Hampshire Line (2,972')		0.0	

Side labels: Maine 11 · Maine Section 12 · Maine Section 13 · Maine Map 7 · Maine Appalachian Trail Club · Appalachian Mountain Club

GBS	N to S	Features	Facilities (see page 8 for codes)	S to N	Map

Miles from Maine–N.H. Line

Miles from Vt.–Mass. Line

	N to S	Features	Facilities	S to N	
N.H Section 1	0.0	Maine–New Hampshire Line (2,972')		310.7	**N.H.–Vt. Map 1**
	1.9	Mt. Success (3,565')		308.8	
	4.7	Gentian Pond Shelter/Campsite (2,166')	CSw	306.0	
	5.4	Moss Pond	w	305.3	
	6.9	Dream Lake	w	303.8	
	9.6	Trident Col Tentsite (2,020')	Cw	301.1	
	10.7	Cascade Mountain (2,631')		300.0	
	15.0	Brook	w	295.7	
	16.2	Androscoggin River (750')	R	294.5	
	16.5	U.S. 2; **Gorham, N.H., P.O. 03581** (w on A.T.; P.O.,G,L,M 3.6m W; C,L,M 1.8m W)	RCGLMw	294.2	
N.H. Section 2	18.4	Rattle River Shelter	Sw	292.3	
	22.4	Mt. Moriah (4,049')		288.3	
	24.5	Imp Shelter/Campsite (3,250')	CSw	286.2	
	27.0	Middle Carter Mountain (4,610')		283.7	
	29.1	Zeta Pass (3,890')		281.6	
	30.5	Carter Dome (4,832')		280.2	
	31.0	Spring	w	279.7	
	31.7	Carter Notch, Carter Notch Hut (3,350') (L,M,w 0.2m E)	LMw	279.0	**N.H.–Vt. Map 2**
	32.6	Wildcat Mountain, Peak A (4,422')		278.1	
	34.6	Wildcat Mountain, Peak D		276.1	
N.H. Section 3	37.6	Pinkham Notch, N.H. 16, Pinkham Notch Camp (2,050') (L,M,w on A.T.)	RLMw	273.1	
	39.7	Low's Bald Spot (2,860')		271.0	
	41.6	West Branch, Peabody River (2,300')	w	269.1	
	42.4	Osgood Tentsite	Cw	268.3	
	44.9	Mt. Madison (5,366')		265.8	

Appalachian Mountain Club

New Hampshire–Vermont

	N to S	Features	Facilities	S to N	
		Miles from *Maine–N.H. Line*		*Miles from* *Vt.–Mass. Line*	
	45.4	Madison Spring Hut, Valley Way Tentsite (C,w 0.6m W; L,M,w on A.T.)	CLMw	265.3	
	46.3	Thunderstorm Junction, Spur Trail to Crag Camp Cabin, Lowe's Path to Mt. Adams & Gray Knob Cabin (S,w 1.1m W, 1.2m W)	Sw	264.4	
	46.9	Israel Ridge Path to The Perch Shelter (C,S,w 0.9m W)	CSw	263.8	
	47.6	Edmands Col (4,938')		263.1	
	51.1	**Mt. Washington, N.H., P.O. 03589** (6,288') (P.O.,M on A.T.)	RM	259.6	
	52.5	Lakes of the Clouds Hut (5,012') (L,M,w on A.T.)	LMw	258.2	
	53.6	Mt. Franklin		257.1	
	54.2	Spring	w	256.5	
	55.5	Spring	w	255.2	
	56.4	Mt. Pierce (Mt. Clinton)		254.3	
	57.2	Mizpah Spring Hut, Nauman Tentsite (3,800') (C,L,M,w on A.T.)	CLMw	253.5	
	58.9	Mt. Jackson		251.8	
	60.3	Mt. Webster (3,910')		250.4	
	63.5	Saco River		247.2	
	63.6	Crawford Notch, U.S. 302, Dry River Campground (1,275') (C 1.8m E; M 1m W; C,G,L 3m E; L,M 3.7m W)	RCGLM	247.1	
	66.5	Ethan Pond Shelter/Campsite (2,860')	CSw	244.2	
	71.3	Zealand Falls Hut (2,630') (L,M,w on A.T.)	LMw	239.4	

Left margin: N.H. Section 3 / N.H. Section 4

Right margin: Randolph Mountain Club / Appalachian Mountain Club / N.H.–Vt. Map 2 / Map 3

New Hampshire–Vermont

GBS	N to S	Features	Facilities (see page 8 for codes)	S to N	Map

Miles from Maine–N.H. Line

Miles from Vt.–Mass. Line

	N to S	Features	Facilities	S to N	
	72.5	Zeacliff		238.2	
	75.5	Mt. Guyot, Guyot Shelter/Campsite (4,580') (C,S,w 0.8m E)	CSw	235.2	
	77.5	South Twin Mountain, North Twin Spur (4,902')		233.2	
	78.3	Galehead Hut (L,M,w on A.T.)	LMw	232.4	
	81.0	Garfield Ridge Shelter/Campsite (3,900')	CSw	229.7	
	81.4	Mt. Garfield (4,500')		229.3	
	84.9	Mt. Lafayette, Greenleaf Hut (5,260') (L,M 1.1m W; w 0.2m W)	LMw	225.8	
	85.9	Mt. Lincoln		224.8	
	86.6	Little Haystack Mountain		224.1	
	88.7	Liberty Spring Tentsite (3,870')	Cw	222.0	
	91.3	Franconia Notch, U.S. 3, Lafayette Place Campground (1,450'); **North Woodstock, N.H., P.O. 03262** (P.O.,G,L,M 5.8m E; G,L,M 2.2m E; C 2.5m W; L 1.6m E)	RCGLM	219.4	
	94.2	Lonesome Lake Hut (2,760') (L,M,w on A.T.)	LMw	216.5	
	96.1	Kinsman Pond Shelter/Campsite	CSw	214.6	
	96.7	North Kinsman Mountain		214.0	
	97.6	South Kinsman Mountain (4,358')		213.1	
	100.1	Eliza Brook Shelter/Campsite (2,400')	CSw	210.6	
	103.0	Mt. Wolf (East Peak) (3,478')		207.7	
	107.6	Kinsman Notch, N.H. 112 (1,870')	R	203.1	
	109.1	Beaver Brook Shelter (3,750')	Sw	201.6	
	111.4	Mt. Moosilauke (4,802')		199.3	
	116.0	Jeffers Brook Shelter (1,350')	Sw	194.7	

GBS column labels (left margin, top to bottom): N.H. Section 4 | N.H. Section 5 | Appalachian Mountain Club | N.H. 6 | DOC

Map column labels (right margin): N.H.–Vt. Map 3 | Map 4

New Hampshire–Vermont

GBS	N to S	Features	Facilities (see page 8 for codes)	S to N	Map

Miles from Maine–N.H. Line

Miles from Vt.–Mass. Line

	N to S	Features	Facilities	S to N	
N.H. Section 7	117.1	N.H. 25 (1,000'); **Glencliff, N.H., P.O. 03238** (P.O.,L 0.5m E)	RL	193.6	
	119.5	Mt. Mist (2,200')		191.2	
	122.0	N.H. 25C (1,550'); **Warren, N.H., P.O. 03279** (w on A.T.; P.O.,G,M 4m E)	RGMw	188.7	
	124.6	Ore Hill Campsite	Cw	186.1	
	125.2	Cape Moonshine Road	R	185.5	
N.H. Section 8	126.8	N.H. 25A (900'); **Wentworth, N.H., P.O. 03282** (P.O.,G,L 4.3m E)	RG	183.9	N.H.–Vt. Map 4
	130.1	Side trail to Mt. Cube (North Summit) (2,911')		180.6	
	131.7	Hexacuba Shelter (w on A.T.; S 0.3m E)	Sw	179.0	
	133.1	South Jacob's Brook (1,450')	w	177.6	
	137.0	Firewarden's Cabin (3,230')	Sw	173.7	
	137.1	Smarts Mountain Tentsite	Cw	173.6	
	140.8	Lyme–Dorchester Road	Rw	169.9	
N.H. Section 9	142.8	Dartmouth Skiway (880'); **Lyme, N.H., P.O. 03768** (P.O.,G,L,M 3.2m W)	RGLM	167.9	N.H.–Vt. Map 5
	143.7	Trapper John Shelter (S,w 0.2m W)	Sw	167.0	
	144.2	Holts Ledge (1,930')		166.5	
	146.2	Goose Pond Road (952')	R	164.5	
	147.5	South Fork Hewes Brook	w	163.2	
	149.4	Moose Mountain Shelter	Sw	161.3	
	150.2	Moose Mountain (South Peak) (2,290')		160.5	

Dartmouth Outing Club (DOC)

New Hampshire–Vermont

GBS	N to S	Features	Facilities (see page 8 for codes)	S to N	Map
		Miles from *Maine–N.H. Line*		*Miles from* *Vt.–Mass. Line*	
	151.8	Mink Brook	w	158.9	
	152.0	Three Mile Road	R	158.7	
	154.5	Etna–Hanover Center Road (845');			
		Etna, N.H., P.O. 03750			
		(P.O. 1.2m E)	R	156.2	
	155.9	Trescott Road	R	154.8	
	158.4	Ledyard Spring			
		(w 0.2m W)	w	152.3	
	158.9	Velvet Rocks Shelter			
		(S 0.2m W)	S	151.8	
	159.7	N.H. 120	R	151.0	
	160.4	Dartmouth College;			
		Hanover, N.H., P.O. 03755	☆		
		(P.O.,G,L,M on A.T.)	RGLM	150.3	
	160.9	New Hampshire–Vermont Line,			
		Connecticut River (400')	R	149.8	
	161.9	**Norwich, Vt., P.O. 05055**	☆		
		(P.O.,G,L,M 0.3m W)	RGLM	148.8	
	166.2	Happy Hill Shelter/Campsite (1,460')	CSw	144.5	
	168.8	Podunk Brook, Podunk Road	Rw	141.9	
	169.6	Tigertown Road, Podunk Road	R	141.1	
	170.2	Vt. 14, White River (400');			
		West Hartford, Vt., P.O. 05084			
		(G,M on A.T.; P.O. 0.3m E)	RGMw	140.5	
	173.5	Joe Ranger Road	R	137.2	
	175.0	Thistle Hill Shelter	Sw	135.7	
	175.3	Thistle Hill (1,800')		135.4	
	177.3	Cloudland Road	R	133.4	
	179.1	Pomfret–South Pomfret Road	Rw	131.6	

Left margin labels: *Green Mountain Club* · *Dartmouth Outing Club (DOC)* · N.H. Section 9 · Vt. Section 1 · Vt. Section 2

Right margin label: N.H.–Vt. Map 5

New Hampshire–Vermont

GBS	N to S	Features	Facilities (see page 8 for codes)	S to N	Map

	Miles from Maine–N.H. Line			*Miles from Vt.–Mass. Line*	
	181.3	Woodstock Stage Road (820'); **South Pomfret, Vt., P.O. 05067** (w on A.T.; P.O.,G 0.9m E)	RGw	129.4	
	182.8	Vt. 12 (882'); **Woodstock, Vt., P.O. 05091** (P.O.,G,L,M 4.4m E)	RGLM	127.9	
	186.6	Wintturi Shelter (1,900') (S,w 0.2m W)	Sw	124.1	
	189.0	Side trail to The Lookout		121.7	
	191.8	Chateauguay Road	R	118.9	
	196.5	Stony Brook Shelter (1,760')	Sw	114.2	
	200.8	River Road (1,214')	R	109.9	
	201.3	Thundering Brook Road	R	109.4	
	202.5	Kent Pond (L,M,w on A.T.)	RLMw	108.2	
	203.2	Vt. 100, Gifford Woods State Park	RCSw	107.5	
	204.6	Sherburne Pass Trail (2,440')		106.1	
	205.5	Junction with Long Trail		105.2	
	206.5	U.S. 4 (1,880'); **Killington, Vt., P.O. 05751** (P.O.,G 2.2m E; L,M 0.9m E)	RGLM	104.2	
	208.4	Churchill Scott Shelter	CSw	102.3	
	210.3	Sherburne Pass Trail, Pico Camp (3,480') (S,w 0.5m E)	Sw	100.4	
	212.8	Cooper Lodge, Killington Peak Trail (3,900') (C,S,w on A.T.; M 0.2m E)	CMSw	97.9	
	217.1	Governor Clement Shelter (1,850')	Sw	93.6	
	218.5	Upper Cold River Road	Rw	92.2	
	219.2	Gould Brook (1,480')	w	91.5	

Left margin labels: Vt. 2 · Vt. Section 3 · Vt. Section 4

Right margin labels: N.H.–Vt. Map 5 · N.H.–Vt. Map 6 · Green Mountain Club

New Hampshire–Vermont

	Miles from Maine–N.H. Line			Miles from Vt.–Mass. Line	
Vt. Section 4	220.0	Cold River Road (Lower Road)	R	90.7	
	222.0	Lottery Road	R	88.7	
	222.4	Beacon Hill		88.3	
	222.9	Clarendon Shelter	CSw	87.8	
	223.9	Vt. 103 (860'); **North Clarendon, Vt., P.O. 05759** (P.O. 4.2m W; M 0.5m W; G 1m W)	RGM	86.8	**N.H.–Vt. Map 6**
	224.0	Clarendon Gorge, Mill River Suspension Bridge	w	86.7	
	226.6	Minerva Hinchey Shelter (1,530')	CSw	84.1	
Vt. Section 5	230.2	Vt. 140 (1,160'); **Wallingford, Vt., P.O. 05773** (w on A.T.; P.O.,G,L,M 2.7m W; G 3.7m E)	RGLMw	80.5	
	230.3	Sugar Hill Road	R	80.4	
	231.7	Greenwall Shelter (S,w 0.2m E)	Sw	79.0	
	232.2	Trail to White Rocks Cliff (2,400')		78.5	
	236.2	Green Mountain Trail to Homer Stone Brook Trail		74.5	**N.H.–Vt. Map 7**
	236.4	Spring	w	74.3	
	236.5	Little Rock Pond Shelter and Tenting Area	CSw	74.2	
Vt. Section 6	238.5	Danby–Landgrove Road (USFS 10), Black Branch (1,500'); **Danby, Vt., P.O. 05739** (P.O.,G,L,M 3.2m W)	RGLM	72.2	
	239.8	Big Branch Shelter	CSw	70.9	
	240.0	Old Job Trail to Old Job Shelter (C,S,w 1m E)	CSw	70.7	
	241.5	Lost Pond Shelter	CSw	69.2	
	243.5	Baker Peak (2,850')		67.2	

Green Mountain Club

New Hampshire–Vermont

GBS	N to S	Features	Facilities (see page 8 for codes)	S to N	Map

Miles from Maine–N.H. Line

Miles from Vt.–Mass. Line

245.5	Griffith Lake (north end)	w	65.2
245.7	Griffith Lake Tenting Area	Cw	65.0
246.2	Peru Peak Shelter	CSw	64.5
247.5	Peru Peak (3,429')		63.2
249.2	Styles Peak		61.5
250.8	Mad Tom Notch, USFS 21 (2,446'); **Peru, Vt., P.O. 05152** (P.O.,G 4m E; C 2.5m E)	RCGw	59.9
253.3	Bromley Mountain (3,260')		57.4
254.3	Bromley Shelter	CSw	56.4
256.3	Vt. 11 & 30 (1,840'); **Manchester Center, Vt., P.O. 05255** (P.O.,G,L,M 5.8m W; G 2.5m E; L,M 2.1m E, 2.7m E)	RGLM	54.4
258.7	Spruce Peak		52.0
259.1	Spruce Peak Shelter	CSw	51.6
261.2	Old Rootville Road, Prospect Rock	R	49.5
262.1	Branch Pond Trail to William B. Douglas Shelter (S,w 0.5m W)	Sw	48.6
264.9	Winhall River	w	45.8
266.8	Stratton Pond, North Shore Trail to North Shore Tenting Area (2,555') (w on A.T.; C,w 0.5m W)	Cw	43.9
267.0	Stratton Pond Trail, Stratton Pond Shelter	Sw	43.7
270.0	Stratton Mountain (3,936') (G,M 1.7m E)	GM	40.7
273.8	Stratton–Arlington Road (Kelley Stand Road) (2,230')	Rw	36.9

*Left margin:* Vt. Section 6 — Vt. Section 7

Right margin: N.H.–Vt. Map 7 — Green Mountain Club

New Hampshire–Vermont

GBS	N to S	Features	Facilities (see page 8 for codes)	S to N	Map
	Miles from Maine–N.H. Line		*Miles from Vt.–Mass. Line*		
	277.4	Story Spring Shelter	CSw	33.3	
	278.3	South Alder Brook	w	32.4	
	282.0	Kid Gore Shelter, Caughnawaga Tentsites	CSw	28.7	
	286.0	Glastenbury Mountain (3,748')		24.7	
	286.3	Goddard Shelter	Sw	24.4	
	288.8	Glastenbury Lookout		21.9	
	290.6	Little Pond Lookout (3,060')		20.1	
	293.2	Hell Hollow Brook	w	17.5	
	294.8	Melville Nauheim Shelter	Sw	15.9	
	296.4	City Stream, Vt. 9 (1,360'); **Bennington, Vt., P.O. 05201** (P.O.,G,L,M 5m W; L 2.7m E; G 3.9m W)	RGLMw	14.3	
	298.2	Harmon Hill (2,325')		12.5	
	300.7	Congdon Shelter	CSw	10.0	
	304.9	Roaring Branch	w	5.8	
	307.6	County Road	R	3.1	
	307.9	Seth Warner Shelter and Primitive Camping Area (C,S,w 0.2m W)	CSw	2.8	
	310.3	Brook	w	0.4	
	310.7	Vermont–Massachusetts Line, southern end of Long Trail (2,330')		0.0	

Vt. Section 8
Vt. Section 9
Green Mountain Club
N.H.–Vt. Map 8

	Miles from Vt.–Mass. Line			Miles from Conn.–N.Y. Line	
Mass. Sec. 1	0.0	Vermont–Massachusetts Line, southern end of Long Trail (2,330')		141.1	
	0.8	Eph's Lookout		140.3	
	1.3	Pine Cobble Trail		139.8	
	2.3	Sherman Brook Primitive Campsite	Cw	138.8	
	4.1	Mass. 2 (650'); **North Adams, Mass., P.O. 01247; Williamstown, Mass., P.O. 01267** (P.O.,G,L,M 2.5m E, 2.9m W; G,M 0.6m E; G,L,M 0.4m W)	RGLM	137.0	
Mass. Section 2	5.0	Pattison Road	Rw	136.1	
	7.1	Wilbur Clearing Shelter (2,300') (C,S,w 0.3m W)	CSw	134.0	**Mass.–Conn. Map 1**
	7.2	Notch Road	R	133.9	
	10.4	Mt. Greylock, Summit Road, Bascom Lodge (3,491') (L,M,w on A.T.)	RLMw	130.7	
	10.9	Notch Road, Rockwell Road	R	130.2	
	13.1	Jones Nose Trail		128.0	
	13.7	Mark Noepel Shelter (2,800') (C,S,w 0.2m E)	CSw	127.4	
	14.6	Old Adams Road		126.5	
	17.3	Outlook Avenue	R	123.8	
Mass. Section 3	18.1	Mass. 8 (1,000'); **Cheshire, Mass., P.O. 01225** (L 0.8m E)	RGLM	123.0	
	18.6	Church Street, School Street (P.O., M, w on A.T.; L 0.1m W)	RLMw	122.5	
	20.0	The Cobbles		121.1	
	22.5	Gore Pond (2,050')		118.6	

AMC Berkshire Chapter

Massachusetts–Connecticut

	Miles from Vt.–Mass. Line			*Miles from Conn.–N.Y. Line*	
	22.9	Crystal Mountain Campsite (C,w 0.2m E)		Cw	118.2
	26.6	Gulf Road		R	114.5
	27.6	Mass. 8, Mass. 9 (1,200'); **Dalton, Mass., P.O. 01226** (M on A.T.; P.O.,G,L,M 0.3m W)		RL	113.5
	28.2	CSX Railroad			112.9
	30.3	Grange Hall Road		R	110.8
	30.6	Kay Wood Shelter (S,w 0.2m E)		Sw	110.5
	33.3	Warner Hill (2,050')			107.8
	34.0	Blotz Road		R	107.1
	35.2	Stream		w	105.9
	37.2	Pittsfield Road (Washington Mountain Road); (G,L 4.6m E; M 1.8m E)		RGLM	103.9
	38.7	West Branch Road		R	102.4
	39.4	October Mountain Shelter (1,950')		CSw	101.7
	41.0	Bald Top			100.1
	41.2	County Road		R	99.9
	43.5	Finerty Pond		w	97.6
	45.3	Becket Mountain (2,180')			95.8
	45.8	Tyne Road		R	95.3
	46.6	U.S. 20 (1,400'); **Lee, Mass., P.O. 01238** (P.O.,G,L,M 5m W)		RGLM	94.5
	46.9	Greenwater Brook		w	94.2
	47.0	Massachusetts Turnpike			94.1
	48.2	Upper Goose Pond Cabin (C,S,w 0.5m W)		CSw	92.9
	49.0	Upper Goose Pond			92.1

AMC Berkshire Chapter

Mass. 3 · Mass. Section 4 · Mass. Section 5 · Mass. Section 6

Mass.–Conn. Map 1 · Mass.–Conn. Map 2

Massachusetts–Connecticut

GBS	N to S	Features	Facilities (see page 8 for codes)	S to N	Map

Miles from Vt.–Mass. Line

Miles from Conn.–N.Y. Line

	N to S	Features	Facilities	S to N	
Mass. 6	50.9	Goose Pond Road	R	90.2	
	53.3	Webster Road (1,800')	Rw	87.8	
	55.2	Tyringham Main Road (930')	R	85.9	
	56.3	Jerusalem Road	RLw	84.8	
		Tyringham, Mass., P.O. 01264			
		(P.O., L 0.6m W)			
Mass. Section 7	58.1	Shaker Campsite	Cw	83.0	
	58.4	Fernside Road			
		(w 0.2m W)	Rw	82.7	
	61.6	Beartown Mountain Road	Rw	79.5	
	62.2	Mt. Wilcox North Shelter (2,100')			
		(S,w 0.3m E)	Sw	78.9	
	64.0	Mt. Wilcox South Shelter	Sw	77.1	
	64.7	The Ledges		76.4	
	65.3	Benedict Pond			
		(C,w 0.5m w)	RCw	75.8	
	66.1	Blue Hill Road (Stony Brook Road)	R	75.0	
	67.3	Mass. 23 (1,000');			
Mass. Section 8		**Great Barrington, Mass., P.O. 01230**	☆		
		(P.O.,G,L,M 4m W)	RGLM	73.8	
	68.2	Lake Buel Road			
		(L,M 2.5m W)	RLM	72.9	
	69.3	Ice Gulch, Tom Leonard Shelter			
		(S on A.T.; w 0.2m E)	Sw	71.8	
	71.4	East Mountain (1,800')	w	69.7	
	72.8	Homes Road	R	68.3	
	74.8	Housatonic River	R	66.3	
	75.7	U.S. 7; **Sheffield, Mass., P.O. 01257**			
		(P.O.,G,L,M 3.3m E; M 0.1m W, 0.8m E)	RGLM	65.4	

Mass.–Conn. Map 2

AMC Berkshire Chapter

Massachusetts–Connecticut

GBS	N to S	Features	Facilities (see page 8 for codes)	S to N	Map
		Miles from Vt.–Mass. Line	*Miles from Conn.–N.Y. Line*		
	77.5	South Egremont Road (700')	R	63.6	
	79.3	Mass. 41; **South Egremont, Mass., P.O. 01258** (P.O.,G,M 1.2m W)	RGM	61.8	
	80.2	Jug End Road (Curtiss Road) (w 0.3m E)	Rw	60.9	
	81.3	Jug End (1,750')		59.8	
	83.0	Elbow Trail		58.1	
	83.6	Glen Brook Shelter	CSw	57.5	
	83.7	The Hemlocks Shelter	Sw	57.4	
	84.1	Guilder Pond Picnic Area	R	57.0	
	84.8	Mt. Everett (2,602')		56.3	
	85.5	Race Brook Falls Trail (C,w 0.4m E)	Cw	55.6	
	86.6	Race Mountain		54.5	
	88.4	Laurel Ridge Campsite	Cw	52.7	
	89.7	Sages Ravine (1,340')	w	51.4	
	90.3	Sages Ravine Brook Campsite	Cw	50.8	
	90.4	Massachusetts–Connecticut Line		50.7	
	91.1	Bear Mountain (2,316')		50.0	
	91.8	Bear Mountain Road	R	49.3	
	92.0	Riga Junction, Undermountain Trail		49.1	
	92.5	Brassie Brook (South Branch), Brassie Brook Shelter	CSw	48.6	
	93.1	Ball Brook Campsite	Cw	48.0	
	93.7	Riga Shelter	CSw	47.4	
	94.4	Lions Head (1,738')		46.7	
	97.1	Conn. 41 (Undermountain Road); **Salisbury, Conn., P.O. 06068** (P.O.,G,L,M 0.8m W)	RGLM	44.0	

Left margin labels: AMC Berkshire Chapter — Mass. 9, Mass. Section 10; AMC Connecticut Chapter — Conn. Section 1

Right margin labels: Mass.–Conn. Map 3

Massachusetts–Connecticut

GBS	N to S	Features	Facilities (see page 8 for codes)	S to N	Map
	Miles from Vt.–Mass. Line			*Miles from Conn.–N.Y. Line*	
	97.8	U.S. 44 (700')	R	43.3	
	100.3	Billy's View		40.8	
	101.1	Rand's View		40.0	
	101.2	Side trail to Limestone Spring Shelter (C,S,w 0.5m W)	CSw	39.9	
	101.9	Prospect Mountain (1,475')		39.2	
	103.3	Spring	w	37.8	
	103.8	Housatonic River Road	R	37.3	
	104.4	Iron Bridge over Housatonic River; **Falls Village, Conn., P.O. 06031** (P.O. 0.5m E)	R	36.7	
	106.3	Mohawk Trail (L 0.2m E)	L	34.8	
	106.4	U.S. 7, Housatonic River (500')	R	34.7	
	107.0	U.S. 7, Conn. 112	R	34.1	
	107.4	Belter's Campsite	Cw	33.7	
	110.2	Sharon Mountain Campsite	Cw	30.9	
	111.4	Mt. Easter (1,350')		29.7	
	111.7	Sharon Mountain Road	R	29.4	
	112.6	Pine Swamp Brook Shelter	CSw	28.5	
	113.7	West Cornwall Road (800'); **West Cornwall, Conn., P.O. 06796** (P.O.,M 2.2m E)	RM	27.4	
	113.8	Carse Brook	w	27.3	
	116.0	Caesar Road, Caesar Brook Campsite	C	25.1	
	116.4	Pine Knob Loop Trail		24.7	
	117.1	Hatch Brook		24.0	
	118.3	Old Sharon Road	R	22.8	
	118.5	Conn. 4; **Cornwall Bridge, Conn., P.O. 06754** (P.O.,G,L 0.9m E)	RGL	22.6	

GBS side labels: Conn. Section 2 · Conn. Section 3

Map side labels: Mass.–Conn. Map 3 · AMC Connecticut Chapter

Massachusetts–Connecticut

	N to S	Features	Facilities	S to N	
	Miles from Vt.–Mass. Line		*Miles from Conn.–N.Y. Line*		
	119.4	Silver Hill Campsite (1,000')	Cw	21.7	
	120.2	River Road	Rw	20.9	
	122.2	Stony Brook Campsite	Cw	18.9	
	122.6	Stewart Hollow Brook Shelter (400')	CSw	18.5	
	124.9	River Road	R	16.2	
	125.4	St. Johns Ledges		15.7	
	126.1	Caleb's Peak (1,160')		15.0	
	126.8	Skiff Mountain Road	R	14.3	
	129.6	Conn. 341, Schaghticoke Road (350'); **Kent, Conn., P.O. 06757** (P.O.,G,L,M 0.8m E)	RGLM	11.5	
	129.9	Mt. Algo Shelter	CSw	11.2	
	130.9	Thayer Brook		10.2	
	132.8	Schaghticoke Mountain Campsite	Cw	8.3	
	133.4	Indian Rocks		7.7	
	133.8	Connecticut–New York Line (1,250')		7.3	
	135.0	Schaghticoke Mountain		6.1	
	136.7	Schaghticoke Road	R	4.4	
	137.4	Side trail to Bulls Bridge Road Parking Area (R 0.2m E; G,M 0.4m E)	RGM	3.7	
	138.1	Ten Mile River (280')	Cw	3.0	
	138.3	Ten Mile River Shelter	S	2.8	
	139.3	Ten Mile Hill (1,000')		1.8	
	140.4	Conn. 55	R	0.7	
	141.1	Hoyt Road, Connecticut–New York Line (400'); **Wingdale, N.Y., P.O. 12594** (P.O.,G,M 3.3m W; M 1.5m W, 2.3m W)	RGM	0.0	

Left margin (bottom to top): New York–New Jersey Trail Conference — AMC Connecticut Chapter — Conn. Section 5 (N.Y. Section 1) — Conn. Section 4

*Right margin:* Mass.–Conn. Map 4

GBS	N to S	Features	Facilities (see page 8 for codes)	S to N	Map

Miles from Conn.–N.Y. Line

Miles from Delaware Water Gap, Pa.

	0.0	Hoyt Road, Connecticut–New York Line (400'); **Wingdale, N.Y., P.O. 12594** (P.O.,G,M 3.3m W; M 1.5m W, 3.3m W)	RGM	161.9
	1.0	Duell Hollow Road	R	160.9
	1.2	Wiley Shelter	Sw	160.7
	1.6	Leather Hill Road (750')	R	160.3
	6.7	Hurds Corners Road	R	155.2
	6.9	N.Y. 22, Metro-North Railroad, Appalachian Trail Railroad Station (480') (G 0.6m E; L 2.6m W; M 2.8m W)	RGLM	155.0
	9.3	County 20 (West Dover Road); **Pawling, N.Y., P.O. 12564** ☆ (P.O.,C,G,M 3.1m E; C 3.1m E)	RCGM	152.6
	10.0	Telephone Pioneers Shelter	Sw	151.9
	10.3	West Mountain (1,200')		151.6
	14.5	N.Y. 55 (720'); **Poughquag, N.Y., P.O. 12570** (P.O.,M 3.1m W; G 3.6m W; M 1.5m W; L 2.6m W)	RGLM	147.4
	14.8	Old Route 55	R	147.1
	16.7	Depot Hill Road	R	145.2
	17.8	Morgan Stewart Shelter	Sw	144.1
	17.9	Mt. Egbert (1,329')		144.0
	20.3	Stormville Mountain Road, I-84	R	141.6
	21.7	N.Y. 52 (800'); **Stormville, N.Y., P.O. 12582** (P.O. 1.7m W; G 0.5m E, 2.2m W, 2.4m W; G,M 2m E)	RGM	140.2
	23.3	Hosner Mountain Road	R	138.6

N.Y. Section 2 · N.Y. Section 3 · N.Y. Section 4 · N.Y. 5

Right margin: N.Y.–N.J. Map 1 · *New York–New Jersey Trail Conference*

New York–New Jersey

Miles from Conn.–N.Y. Line *Miles from Delaware Water Gap, Pa.*

	N to S	Features	Facilities	S to N	
	26.5	Taconic State Parkway	R	135.4	
	26.8	Hortontown Road, RPH Shelter (350')	RSw	135.1	
	28.1	Shenandoah Tenting Area	Cw	133.8	
	29.2	Long Hill Road	R	132.7	
	29.6	Shenandoah Mountain (1,282')		132.3	
	33.8	N.Y. 301, Canopus Lake, Fahnestock State Park (C,w 1m E)	RCw	128.1	
	35.9	Sunk Mine Road (800')	R	126.0	
	37.5	Dennytown Road	RCw	124.4	
	40.2	South Highland Road	R	121.7	
	41.2	Canopus Hill Road (420')	R	120.7	
	42.9	Old Albany Post Road, Chapman Road	R	119.0	
	43.7	Denning Hill (900')		118.2	
	45.6	Old West Point Road, Graymoor Friary	R	116.3	
	46.2	U.S. 9, N.Y. 403 (400'); **Peekskill, N.Y., P.O. 10566** (P.O.,G,L,M 4.8m E; M 0.7m E; G on A.T.)	RGLM	115.7	
	49.6	South Mountain Pass (Manitou Road)	R	112.3	
	49.8	Hemlock Springs Campsite	Cw	112.1	
	50.8	Camp Smith Trail, Anthony's Nose (700')		111.1	
	51.3	N.Y. 9D	R	110.6	
	52.0	Bear Mountain Bridge; **Fort Montgomery, N.Y., P.O., 10922** (P.O.,G,L,M, 0.7m W)	RGLM	109.9	
	52.1	Trailside Museum and Zoo (124')		109.8	
	52.8	Bear Mountain Inn, **Bear Mountain, N.Y., P.O. 10911** (P.O. 0.3m E; L,M,w on A.T.)	RLMw	109.1	
	54.8	Bear Mountain (1,305')	Rw	107.1	

Left margin (vertical): New York–New Jersey Trail Conference

*Left margin sections (top to bottom):* N.Y. Section 6 · N.Y. Section 7 · N.Y. 8 · N.Y. Section 9 · N.Y. Section 10

*Right margin (vertical):* N.Y.–N.J. Map 1 · N.Y.–N.J. Map 2

New York–New Jersey

Miles from
Conn.–N.Y. Line

Miles from
Delaware Water Gap, Pa.

	N to S	Features	Facilities	S to N
	57.2	Seven Lakes Drive	R	104.7
	59.0	Trail to West Mountain Shelter		
		(S 0.6m E)	S(nw)	102.9
	59.8	Beechy Bottom Brook	w	102.1
	60.0	Palisades Interstate Parkway (680')	R	101.9
	60.7	Black Mountain (1,160')		101.2
	62.1	William Brien Memorial Shelter	S(nw)	99.8
	63.3	Goshen Mountain		98.6
	64.1	Seven Lakes Drive	R	97.8
	66.3	Arden Valley Road (1,196')		
		(w 0.3m E)	Rw	95.6
	67.4	Fingerboard Shelter	S(nw)	94.5
	68.4	Surebridge Mountain		93.5
	69.5	Lemon Squeezer		92.4
	70.1	Island Pond Outlet	w	91.8
	71.4	Arden Valley Road	R	90.5
	71.6	New York State Thruway (560')		90.3
	71.8	N.Y. 17; **Arden, N.Y., P.O. 10910;**		
		Southfields, N.Y., P.O. 10975		
		(P.O. 0.7m W; P.O.,L,M 2.1m E;		
		G 1.8m E, 5.7m E)	RGLM	90.1
	72.9	Arden Mountain (1,180')		89.0
	73.6	Orange Turnpike		
		(w 0.5m E)	Rw	88.3
	74.3	Little Dam Lake		87.6
	75.0	East Mombasha Road	R	86.9
	75.8	Buchanan Mountain (1,142')		86.1
	76.7	West Mombasha Road		
		(G 0.6m W)	RG	85.2
	77.9	Mombasha High Point (1,280')		84.0

Section labels (left margin): N.Y. Section 10, N.Y. Section 11, N.Y. Section 12

Map label (right margin): N.Y.–N.J. Map 2 — *New York–New Jersey Trail Conference*

New York–New Jersey

| GBS | N to S | Features | Facilities (see page 8 for codes) | S to N | Map |

GBS	N to S	Features	Facilities (see page 8 for codes)	S to N	Map
	Miles from Conn.–N.Y. Line			*Miles from Delaware Water Gap, Pa.*	
	79.9	Fitzgerald Falls	w	82.0	
	80.2	Lakes Road (680')	R	81.7	
	81.7	Wildcat Shelter	Sw	80.2	
	82.0	Cat Rocks		79.9	
	82.5	Eastern Pinnacles (1,294')		79.4	
	83.8	N.Y. 17A; **Greenwood Lake, N.Y., P.O. 10925** (G 1.6m W; P.O.,G,L,M 2m E; G,L,M 3.5m W)	RGLM	78.1	
	89.3	Prospect Rock (1,433')		72.6	
	89.7	State Line Trail, New York–New Jersey Line; **Hewitt, N.J., P.O. 07421** (P.O.,G,M 3.7m E)	GM	72.2	
	90.8	Long House Creek		71.1	
	91.9	Long House Road (Brady Road) (G,M 0.7m W)	RGM	70.0	
	93.3	Warwick Turnpike (1,140') (G 1.8m E, 2.7m W; L,M 0.8m W; M 1.5m E)	RGLM	68.6	
	93.8	Wawayanda Shelter (S on A.T.; w 0.4m E)	Sw	68.1	
	94.0	Wawayanda Road	R	67.9	
	94.6	Iron Mountain Road Bridge	R	67.3	
	95.7	Barrett Road; **New Milford, N.Y., P.O. 10959** (P.O.,G 1.8m W)	RG	66.2	
	97.4	Wawayanda Mountain (1,340')		64.5	

Side labels (left): N.Y. Section 12 · N.Y. Section 13 · N.J. Section 1 · New York–New Jersey Trail Conference

Side labels (right): N.Y.–N.J. Map 2 · N.Y.–N.J. Map 3

New York–New Jersey

	Miles from Conn.–N.Y. Line		*Miles from Delaware Water Gap, Pa.*		
	98.8	N.J. 94 (450'); **Vernon, N.J., P.O. 07462** (P.O.,G,M 2.4m E)	RGM	63.1	
	99.7	Canal Road	R	62.2	
	100.4	Pochuck Creek footbridge		61.5	
	101.1	County 517	R	60.8	
	102.6	County 565; **Glenwood, N.J., P.O. 07418** (P.O. 0.7m W; L 1m W)	RL	59.3	
	103.8	Pochuck Mountain (800')		58.1	
	105.3	Pochuck Mountain Shelter	S(nw)	56.6	
	105.8	Lake Wallkill Road (Liberty Corners Road)	Rw	56.1	
	108.1	Wallkill River	R	53.8	
	109.1	Oil City Road	R	52.8	
	109.6	N.J. 284 (420') (G 0.4m W)	RG	52.3	
	110.6	Lott Road; **Unionville, N.Y., P.O. 10988** (P.O.,G,M 0.4m W)	RGM	51.3	
	111.5	Unionville Road	R	50.4	
	113.8	Gemmer Road	R	48.1	
	116.4	County 519	R	45.5	
	117.7	High Point Shelter	Sw	44.2	
	118.2	Side trail to High Point Monument		43.7	
	119.4	N.J. 23 (1,500') (w on A.T.; G 2.5m E, 4.3m W; L 1.4m E, 4.4m W; M 4.3m W)	RGLMw	42.5	
	122.0	Trail to Rutherford Shelter (S,w 0.4m E)	Sw	39.9	
	124.7	Deckertown Turnpike	R	37.2	
	124.9	Mashipacong Shelter	S	37.0	

N.J. Section 2 · N.J. Section 3 · N.J. Section 4

N.Y.–N.J. Map 3

New York–New Jersey Trail Conference

GBS	N to S	Features	Facilities (see page 8 for codes)	S to N	Map
	Miles from Conn.–N.Y. Line		*Miles from Delaware Water Gap, Pa.*		
	127.5	Crigger Road	R	34.4	
	128.3	Sunrise Mountain (1,653')	R	33.6	Map 3
	130.7	Trail to Gren Anderson Shelter	Sw	31.2	
	131.8	Culver Fire Tower		30.1	
	133.7	Culvers Gap, U.S. 206 (935'); **Branchville, N.J., P.O. 07826** (P.O. 3.4m E; G on A.T., 1.6m E; L 2.5m E, 1.9m W; M 0.1m W, 0.6m E)	RGLM	28.2	
	137.3	Brink Road Shelter (S,w 0.2m W)	Sw	24.6	
	139.5	Rattlesnake Mountain (1,492')		22.4	
	141.4	Buttermilk Falls Trail		20.5	
	144.3	Blue Mountain Lakes Road	Rw	17.6	
	148.2	Millbrook–Blairstown Road (1,260')	R	13.7	N.Y.–N.J. Map 4
	148.6	Rattlesnake Spring	w	13.3	
	149.2	Catfish Fire Tower (1,565')		12.7	
	151.6	Camp Road, Mohican Outdoor Center (C,L,w 0.3m W)	RCLw	10.3	
	155.9	Spring	w	6.0	
	156.0	Sunfish Pond (1,382')		5.9	
	157.3	Backpacker Site	C(nw)	4.6	
	158.9	Holly Springs Trail (w 0.2m E)	w	3.0	
	160.5	I-80 Overpass	R	1.4	
	160.9	Delaware Water Gap National Recreation Area Information Center	Rw	1.0	
	161.9	Delaware River Bridge (west end), New Jersey–Pennsylvania Line (350')	R	0.0	

Left margin labels: New York–New Jersey Trail Conference; N.J. 4; N.J. Section 5; N.J. Section 6

Pennsylvania

GBS	N to S	Features	Facilities (see page 8 for codes)	S to N	Map

Miles from
Delaware Water Gap, Pa.

Miles from
Pa.–Md. Line

	0.0	Delaware River Bridge (west end), New Jersey–Pennsylvania Line (350')	R	229.3
	0.2	Pa. 611, **Delaware Water Gap, Pa., P.O. 18327**	☆	
		(P.O.,M 0.1m W; L,M 0.4m W; G,L 3.2m W)	RGLM	229.1
	0.9	Council Rock		228.4
	1.7	Lookout Rock		227.6
	2.7	Mt. Minsi (1,461')		226.6
	4.7	Totts Gap		224.6
	6.6	Kirkridge Shelter (1,500')	Sw	222.7
	7.2	Fox Gap, Pa. 191	R	222.1
	8.3	Wolk Rocks Bypass Trail (north end)		221.0
	8.8	Wolf Rocks (1,643')		220.5
	9.4	Wolk Rocks Bypass Trail (south end)		219.9
	15.8	Pa. 33 (980'); **Wind Gap, Pa., P.O. 18091**		
		(P.O.,G,L,M 1m E; L 0.1m W)	RGLM	213.5
	16.8	Hahns Lookout		212.5
	20.4	Leroy A. Smith Shelter (S 0.1m E; w 0.2m E)	Sw	208.9
	23.9	Smith Gap Road	R	205.4
	24.6	Spring (w 0.6m E)	w	204.7
	26.4	Delps Trail (1,580')		202.9
	31.2	Little Gap (1,100'); **Danielsville, Pa., P.O. 18038** (P.O.,G,M 1.5m E; w 1.2m W)	RGMw	198.1
	36.2	Pa. 248	R	193.1
	36.4	Lehigh River Bridge (east end), Pa. 873 (380'); **Palmerton, Pa., P.O. 18071** (P.O.,G,L,M 2m W)	RGLM	192.9

Pa. Section 1 — Pa. Section 2

Wilmington Trail Club — Batona — AMC Delaware Valley Chapter — Philadelphia TC

KTA Sections 1–6 Map

Pennsylvania

GBS	N to S	Features	Facilities (see page 8 for codes)	S to N	Map

*Miles from
Delaware Water Gap, Pa.*

*Miles from
Pa.–Md. Line*

	36.5	Lehigh Gap, Pa. 873; **Slatington, Pa., P.O. 18080** (P.O.,G,L,M 2m E)	RGLM	192.8	
	37.1	George W. Outerbridge Shelter	Sw	192.2	
	41.5	Ashfield Road, Lehigh Furnace Gap (1,320'); **Ashfield, Pa., P.O. 18212** (P.O.,G 2.2m W; w 0.7m E)	RGw	187.8	
	43.9	Bake Oven Knob Shelter	Sw	185.4	
	44.5	Bake Oven Knob (1,560')		184.8	
	44.9	Bake Oven Knob Road	R	184.4	
	46.3	Bear Rocks		183.0	
	47.0	Knife Edge		182.3	
	48.0	New Tripoli Campsite (C,w 0.2m W)	Cw	181.3	
	49.8	Pa. 309, Blue Mountain Summit (1,360') (L,M,w on A.T.)	RLMw	179.5	
	52.0	Fort Franklin Road	R	177.3	
	53.9	Allentown Hiking Club Shelter	Sw	175.4	
	55.2	Tri-County Corner (1,560')		174.1	
	61.3	Hawk Mountain Road, Eckville Shelter (600') (S,w 0.2m E)	RSw	168.0	
	66.6	The Pinnacle		162.7	
	67.0	Trail to Blue Rocks Campground (C,G,S 1.5m E)	CGS	162.3	
	68.8	Pulpit Rock (1,582')		160.5	
	70.4	Windsor Furnace Shelter (940')	Sw	158.9	
	70.6	Windsor Furnace		158.7	

Side labels (GBS column): Phila. TC; Blue Mtn Eagle; Pa. Section 3; Allentown Hiking Club; Blue Mountain Eagle Climbing Club; Pa. Section 4

Side labels (Map column): KTA Sections 1–6 Map

Pennsylvania

	N to S	Features	Facilities	S to N	
		Miles from *Delaware Water Gap, Pa.*		*Miles from* *Pa.–Md. Line*	
Pa. Section 4	73.2	Pocahontas Spring (1,200') (w on A.T.; L,M 1m E)	LMw	156.1	
	75.8	Pa. 61 (M 0.5m W)	RM	153.5	
	76.5	**Port Clinton, Pa., P.O. 19549** (400') (P.O. on A.T.; L,S 0.5m W; G,M,L 3m E)	RGLMS	152.8	
Pa. Section 5	80.5	Phillip's Canyon Spring (1,500')	w	148.8	
	83.2	Shartlesville Cross-Mountain Road; **Shartlesville, Pa., P.O. 19554** (P.O.,G,L,M 3.6m E)	RGLM	146.1	
	85.1	Eagle's Nest Shelter (S,w 0.3m W)	Sw	144.2	
	85.8	Sand Spring Trail (w 0.2m E)	w	143.5	
	89.6	Black Swatara Spring (w 0.3m E)	w	139.7	
	90.9	Pa. 183, Rentschler Marker (1,440')	R	138.4	
	91.2	Fort Dietrich Snyder Marker (w 0.2m W)	w	138.1	
	94.5	Shuberts Gap		134.8	
	94.6	Hertlein Campsite	Cw	134.7	
Pa. Section 6	97.1	Round Head and Shower Steps	w	132.2	
	99.7	Trail to Pilger Ruh Spring	Cw	129.6	
	100.2	Pa. 501; **Pine Grove, Pa., P.O. 17963,** 501 Shelter (P.O.,M 3.7m W; S,w 0.1m W; G 4.3m W; L 5.7m W)	RGLMSw	129.1	
	102.1	Pa. 645	R	127.2	
	104.3	Blue Mountain Spring, William Penn Shelter (1,380')	Sw	125.0	

KTA Sections 1–6 Map

Blue Mountain Eagle Climbing Club (BMECC)

Pennsylvania

GBS	N to S	Features	Facilities (see page 8 for codes)	S to N	Map
		Miles from Delaware Water Gap, Pa.	*Miles from* Pa.–Md. Line		
	111.2	I-81	R	118.1	
	111.6	Swatara Gap, Pa. 72 (480')			
		(C,G,L,M 2m E)	RGL	117.7	
	113.0	Pa. 443; Green Point, Pa.	R	116.3	
	117.7	Rausch Gap Shelter (980')			
		(S,w 0.3m E)	Sw	111.6	
	120.0	Cold Spring Trail		109.3	
	122.3	Yellow Springs Village Site		107.0	
	125.7	Stony Mountain; Horse-Shoe Trail (1,650')		103.6	
	129.0	Pa. 325, Clarks Valley (550')	Rw	100.3	
	129.3	Spring	w	100.0	
	131.6	Shikellimy Trail		97.7	
	133.0	Kinter View (1,320')		96.3	
	134.7	Victoria Trail		94.6	
	135.7	Peters Mountain Shelter	Sw	93.6	
	136.5	Table Rock		92.8	
	138.5	Pa. 225	R	90.8	
	142.4	Clarks Ferry Shelter (1,260')	Sw	86.9	
	142.6	Campsite	Cw	86.7	
	144.8	U.S. 22 & 322, Norfolk Southern Railway	R	84.5	
	145.4	Clarks Ferry Bridge (west end), Susquehanna River (380')			
		(C on A.T.; M 0.1m W)	RCM	83.9	
	145.6	Juniata River, Pa. 849	R	83.7	
	146.6	**Duncannon, Pa., P.O. 17020**	☆		
		(P.O.,L,M on A.T., G 0.6m W)	RGLM	82.7	
	147.1	U.S. 11 & 15, Pa. 274	R	82.2	
	148.8	Hawk Rock		80.5	
	150.7	Cove Mountain Shelter (1,200')	Sw	78.6	
	155.7	Pa. 850 (650')	R	73.6	

Left margin labels (top to bottom): BMECC · Susquehanna A.T. Club · Pa. Section 7 · Pa. Section 8 · York · Mtn. Club of Maryland · Pa. Section 9

Right margin labels: KTA Sections 7–8 Map · PATC Map 1

Pennsylvania

GBS	N to S	Features	Facilities (see page 8 for codes)	S to N	Map
	Miles from *Delaware Water Gap, Pa.*			*Miles from* *Pa.–Md. Line*	
Pa. 9	158.0	Darlington Shelter (1,250')	Sw	71.3	MCM
	158.1	Darlington Trail, Tuscarora Trail		71.2	
	159.0	Spring	w	70.3	
	160.0	Pa. 944 (480'); Donnellytown, Pa.	R	69.3	
	162.0	Conodoguinet Creek, Scott Farm Trail Work Center	Rw	67.3	
Pa. Section 10	163.4	I-81 Crossing	R	65.9	
	164.3	U.S. 11; **Carlisle, Pa., P.O. 17013** **New Kingston, Pa., P.O. 17072** (P.O. 5m W; 1.7m E; G 1.3m E; L,M 0.3m W; M 0.3m E)	RGLM	65.0	Cumberland Valley A.T. Club
	165.5	Pennsylvania Turnpike	R	63.8	
	168.2	Trindle Road (Pa. 641)	R	61.1	PATC Map 1
	170.3	Pa. 74	R	59.0	
Pa. Section 11	172.3	Pa. 174, ATC Mid-Atlantic Regional Office; **Boiling Springs, Pa., P.O. 17007** (P.O.,w on A.T.; G,L,M 0.1m W; G 1m W)	☆ RGLMw	57.0	
	172.6	Yellow Breeches Creek (500')	R	56.7	
	172.8	Backpackers' Campsite	Cw	56.5	
	175.3	Center Point Knob (1,060')		54.0	
	176.2	Alec Kennedy Shelter	Sw	53.1	
	178.3	Whiskey Spring, Whiskey Spring Road	Rw	51.0	Mtn. Club of Md.
Pa. 12	181.1	Pa. 94 (880'); **Mount Holly Springs, Pa., P.O. 17065** (P.O.,G,M 2.5m W)	RGM	48.2	
	182.9	Hunters Run Road (Pa. 34); **Gardners, Pa., P.O. 17324** (P.O. 5m E; G 0.2m E)	RG	46.4	PATC 2–3

Pennsylvania

GBS	N to S	Features	Facilities (see page 8 for codes)	S to N	Map

Miles from
Delaware Water Gap, Pa.

Miles from
Pa.–Md. Line

	183.8	Pine Grove Road (C,M 0.4m W)	RCM	45.5	
	184.3	James Fry (Tagg Run) Shelter (S,w 0.2m E)	Sw	45.0	
	185.5	Side trail to Mountain Creek Campground (C,G 0.7m W)	CG	43.8	
	185.7	Limekiln Road	R	43.6	
	189.0	Side trail to Pole Steeple (1,300')		40.3	
	191.5	Pine Grove Furnace State Park	RCGLw	37.8	
	191.8	Pa. 233 (900'), Appalachian Trail Museum	R	37.5	
	195.2	Toms Run Shelter (1)	Sw	34.1	
	196.3	Woodrow Road	R	33.0	
	198.2	Michener Cabin (locked) (w 0.3m E)	w	31.1	
	200.1	Shippensburg Road, Big Flat Fire Tower (2,040')	R	29.2	
	201.4	Birch Run Shelter	Sw	27.9	
	203.8	Milesburn Road, Milesburn Cabin (locked)	Rw	25.5	
	204.2	Ridge Road, Means Hollow Road	R	25.1	
	204.7	Middle Ridge Road	R	24.6	
	207.3	Sandy Sod Junction (1,980')	R	22.0	
	208.8	Quarry Gap Shelters	Sw	20.5	
	209.5	Quarry Gap Road	R	19.8	
	211.4	U.S. 30, Caledonia State Park, Thaddeus Stevens Museum (960'); **Fayetteville, Pa., P.O. 17222** (P.O.,G,L,M 3.5m W; C,w on A.T.; M 0.5m W; G 0.9m W)	RCGLMw	17.9	

Left margin (top to bottom): Mountain Club of Maryland — Pa. Section 12 — Potomac A.T. Club — Pa. Section 13

*Right margin:* PATC Maps 2–3

Pennsylvania

GBS	N to S	Features	Facilities (see page 8 for codes)	S to N	Map
		Miles from *Delaware Water Gap, Pa.*	*Miles from* *Pa.–Md. Line*		
Pa. Section 14	214.4	Rocky Mountain Shelters (S 0.2m E; w 0.5m E)	Sw	14.9	PATC Map 4 / Potomac A.T. Club
	216.1	Pa. 233 (1,600'); **South Mountain, Pa., P.O. 17261** (P.O.,G 1.2m E)	RG	13.2	
	216.4	Swamp Road	R	12.9	
	219.7	Chimney Rocks (1,900')		9.6	
	221.0	Tumbling Run Shelters, Hermitage Cabin (locked)	Sw	8.3	
	221.2	Old Forge Road (1,000')	R	8.1	
	221.8	Rattlesnake Run Road	R	7.5	
	222.2	Antietam Shelter, Old Forge Park	RSw	7.1	
	224.6	Deer Lick Shelters (1,420')	Sw	4.7	
	225.9	Bailey Spring	w	3.4	
	226.5	Mackie Run, Mentzer Gap Road	R	2.8	
	226.7	Pa. 16; **Blue Ridge Summit, Pa., P.O. 17214** (P.O.,G,M 1.2m E; G 2.6m W)	RGM	2.6	
	227.0	Old Pa. 16	R	2.3	
	228.2	Buena Vista Road	Rw	1.1	
	229.2	Pen Mar Road	R	0.1	
	229.3	Pennsylvania–Maryland Line (1,250')	R	0.0	

GBS	N to S	Features	Facilities (see page 8 for codes)	S to N	Map

Miles from Pa.–Md. Line — *Miles from Front Royal, Va.*

	N to S	Features	Facilities	S to N	
Md. Section 1	0.0	Pennsylvania–Maryland Line (1,250')	R	94.9	
	0.2	Pen Mar Park; **Cascade, Md., P.O. 21719** (P.O.,G,M 1.6m E; w on A.T.; M 1.4m E)	RGMw	94.7	
	3.1	Trail to High Rock	R	91.8	
	4.9	Raven Rocks Shelter (C,S 0.2m W; w 0.1m E)	CSw	90.0	
Md. Sec. 2	5.9	Raven Rock Hollow, Md. 491	R	89.0	
	6.7	Warner Gap Road	Rw	88.2	
	8.5	Foxville Road (Md. 77)	R	86.4	
	9.8	Ensign Cowall Shelter	Sw	85.1	
Md. Section 3	10.0	Wolfsville Road (Md. 17) (1,400'); **Smithsburg, Md., P.O. 21783** (P.O.,G,M 2.4m W; L 6.4m W)	RGLM	84.9	PATC Maps 5-6
	14.8	Pogo Memorial Campsite	Cw	80.1	
	15.4	Black Rock Cliffs (1,800')		79.5	
	16.4	Trail to Annapolis Rock (C 0.2m W; w 0.4m W)	Cw	78.5	
	18.0	Pine Knob Shelter	CSw	76.9	
Md. Section 4	18.6	I-70 Footbridge, U.S. 40 (C 1.4m W; M,w 0.5m W)	RCMw	76.3	
	19.4	Boonsboro Mountain Road	R	75.5	
	21.5	Washington Monument		73.4	
	21.9	Washington Monument Road	Rw	73.0	
	22.1	Monument Road	R	72.8	
	23.5	Turners Gap, U.S. Alt. 40 (1,000'); **Boonsboro, Md., P.O. 21713** (M on A.T; P.O.,M 2.3m W; G 1.6m W, 3.7m W)	RGM	71.4	

Potomac A.T. Club

Maryland–West Virginia–Northern Virginia

GBS	N to S	Features	Facilities (see page 8 for codes)	S to N	Map
		Miles from Pa.–Md. Line		*Miles from Front Royal, Va.*	
	23.7	Dahlgren Back Pack Campground	Cw	71.2	
	24.5	Reno Monument Road	R	70.4	
Md. Section 5	25.5	Rocky Run Shelter (C,S,w 0.2m W)	CSw	69.4	
	27.1	Lambs Knoll (1,600')		67.8	
	27.3	White Rocks Cliff		67.6	
	27.9	Trail to Bear Spring Cabin (locked) (w 0.5m E)	w	67.0	
	30.5	Crampton Gap Shelter (C,S,w 0.3m E)	CSw	64.4	
Md. Section 6	30.9	Crampton Gap, Gathland State Park, Gapland Road (Md. 572) (950'); **Burkittsville, Md., P.O. 21718** (P.O. 1.2m E; w on A.T.)	Rw	64.0	PATC Maps 5-6
	32.6	Brownsville Gap		62.3	
	34.6	Ed Garvey Shelter (S on A.T.; w 0.4m E)	Sw	60.3	*Potomac A.T. Club*
	36.7	Trail to Weverton Cliffs		58.2	
Md. Section 7	37.6	Weverton Road (G 1.4m W)	RG	57.3	
	37.8	U.S. 340 Underpass		57.1	
	38.0	Keep Tryst Road (L,M 1.2m W)	RLM	56.9	
	38.1	C&O Canal Towpath (east junction)		56.8	
	39.6	U.S. 340, Sandy Hook Bridge		55.3	
	40.7	C&O Canal Towpath (west junction)		54.2	
	40.9	Potomac River, Goodloe Byron Memorial Footbridge, Maryland–West Virginia Line (250')		54.0	

Maryland–West Virginia–Northern Virginia

PATC Map 7

GBS	N to S	Features	Facilities (see page 8 for codes)	S to N	Map
		Miles from Pa.–Md. Line		*Miles from Front Royal, Va.*	
	41.0	Shenandoah Street; Harpers Ferry National Historical Park (M 0.1m W)	RM	53.9	
	41.6	Appalachian Trail Conservancy Side Trail; **Harpers Ferry, W.Va., P.O. 25425** (P.O. 0.5m W; G 1.1m W; L 0.6m W; M 0.4m W; ATC 0.2m W)	☆ RGLM	53.3	
	41.9	U.S. 340, Shenandoah River Bridge (north end) (L 0.1m W; C 1.2m W)	RCL	53.0	
	42.6	Chestnut Hill Road (W.Va. 32)	R	52.3	
	43.3	Loudoun Heights Trail, West Virginia–Virginia Line (1,200')		51.6	
	47.2	Keys Gap, W.Va. 9 (G,M,w 0.3m W, 0.3m E)	RGMw	47.7	
	50.2	David Lesser Memorial Shelter (S 0.1m E; C,w 0.3m E)	CSw	44.7	
	53.4	Trail to Blackburn Trail Center (1,650') (C 0.1m E; S,w 0.3m E)	CSw	41.5	
	54.6	Wilson Gap		40.3	
	57.5	Devils Racecourse		37.4	
	57.6	Sand Spring	w	37.3	
	58.2	Crescent Rock		36.7	
	58.3	West Virginia–Virginia Line		36.6	
	58.6	Spring	w	36.3	

Potomac A.T. Club

W.Va.–Va. Section 1

W.Va.–Va. Section 2

Maryland–West Virginia–Northern Virginia

GBS	N to S	Features	Facilities (see page 8 for codes)	S to N	Map

Miles from Pa.–Md. Line   *Miles from Front Royal, Va.*

	N to S	Features	Facilities	S to N	
Va. Section 3	60.8	Snickers Gap, Va. 7, Va. 679 (1,000'); **Bluemont, Va., P.O. 20135** (P.O. 1.7m E; G 1m W; M 0.3m W, 0.9m W)	RGM	34.1	
	61.4	Bears Den Rocks, Bears Den Hostel (L,w 0.2m E)	Lw	33.5	
	64.4	Sawmill Spring, Sam Moore Shelter	Sw	30.5	
	66.4	Spring	w	28.5	
	67.6	Morgans Mill Road (Va. 605)	R	27.3	
	71.3	Rod Hollow Shelter	Sw	23.6	
Va. Section 4	74.9	Ashby Gap, U.S. 50 (900') (G,M 0.8m W; L 4m W; L,M 1.2m E)	RLM	20.0	
	77.5	Sky Meadows State Park Side Trail (C,w 1.3m E)	Cw	17.4	
	78.7	Spring	w	16.2	
	79.7	Dick's Dome Shelter (S,w 0.2m E)	Sw	15.2	
	82.3	Trillium Trail (1,900')		12.6	
	84.2	Manassas Gap Shelter	Sw	10.7	
Va. Section 5	86.7	Va. 55 (800'); **Linden, Va., P.O. 22642** (P.O.,G 1m W)	RG	8.2	
	88.6	Va. 638	R	6.3	
	89.7	Jim & Molly Denton Shelter	CSw	5.2	
	91.6	Mosby Campsite, Tom Sealock Spring (1,800')	Cw	3.3	
	94.9	U.S. 522 (950'); **Front Royal, Va., P.O. 22630** (P.O.,G 4.2m W; G,M 3.2m W; L,M 3.6m W)	☆ / RGLM	0.0	

PATC Map 8 — Potomac A.T. Club

Shenandoah National Park

GBS	N to S	Features	Facilities (see page 8 for codes)	S to N	Map

Miles from
Front Royal, Va.

Miles from
Rockfish Gap, Va.

	N to S	Features	Facilities	S to N
	0.0	U.S. 522 (950');		
		Front Royal, Va., P.O. 22630	☆	
		(P.O.,G 4.2m W; G,M 3.2m W;		
		L,M 3.6m W)	RGLM	107.8
	1.4	Va. 602	R	106.4
	2.9	Tom Floyd Wayside	Sw	104.9
	3.6	Possums Rest Overlook, SNP boundary; self-registration station for SNP camping permits		104.2
	3.8	Compton Gap Horse Trail		104.0
	5.3	Indian Run Spring		
		(w 0.3m E)	w	102.5
	5.6	Compton Gap; Skyline Drive, mile 10.4	R	102.2
	6.4	Compton Peak (2,909')		101.4
	6.8	Compton Springs	w	101.0
	7.7	Jenkins Gap; Skyline Drive, mile 12.3	R	100.1
	9.4	Hogwallow Gap;		
		Skyline Drive, mile 14.2 (2,739')	R	98.4
	10.0	Hogwallow Spring	w	97.8
	10.9	North Marshall Mountain (3,368')		96.9
	11.6	Skyline Drive, mile 15.9	R	96.2
	12.1	South Marshall Mountain (3,212')		95.7
	13.2	Gravel Springs Gap;		
		Skyline Drive, mile 17.7 (2,666')	R	94.6
	13.4	Gravel Springs Hut		
		(S,w 0.2m E)	Sw	94.4
	14.5	Skyline Drive, mile 18.9	R	93.3
	15.0	Little Hogback Mountain		92.8
	15.1	Little Hogback Overlook;		
		Skyline Drive, mile 19.7	R	92.7

Potomac A.T. Club

SNP Section 1 (Va. 6)

SNP Section 2 (Va.7)

PATC Map 9

Shenandoah National Park

PATC Map 9

PATC Map 10

Potomac A.T. Club

GBS	N to S	Features	Facilities (see page 8 for codes)		S to N	Map
	Miles from Front Royal, Va.				*Miles from Rockfish Gap, Va.*	
	15.8	First peak of Hogback			92.0	
	15.9	Spring (w 0.2m E)		w	91.9	
	16.1	Second peak of Hogback (3,475')			91.7	
	16.3	Skyline Drive, mile 20.8		R	91.5	
	16.4	Third peak of Hogback			91.4	
	16.6	Skyline Drive, mile 21.1		R	91.2	
	17.0	Tuscarora Trail			90.8	
	17.6	Rattlesnake Point Overlook; Skyline Drive, mile 21.9		R	90.2	
	18.3	Range View Cabin (locked) (w 0.1m E)		w	89.5	
	19.1	Elkwallow Gap; Skyline Drive, mile 23.9 (2,480') (G,M 0.1m E)		RGM	88.7	
	19.6	Spring		w	88.2	
	24.2	Byrds Nest #4 Picnic Shelter (0.5m E)		w	83.6	
	24.3	Beahms Gap; Skyline Drive, mile 28.5		R	83.5	
	24.6	Skyline Drive, mile 28.6		R	83.2	
	25.7	Pass Mountain (3,052')			82.1	
	26.5	Pass Mountain Hut (S,w 0.2m E)		Sw	81.3	
	27.7	Thornton Gap, U.S. 211; Skyline Drive, mile 31.5 (2,307')		R	80.1	
	29.6	Marys Rock (3,514')			78.2	
	30.2	Meadow Spring (w 0.3m E)		w	77.6	
	30.9	Byrds Nest #3 Shelter		S	76.9	
	31.9	The Pinnacle (3,730')			75.9	

SNP Section 2 (Va. 7)

SNP Section 3 (Va. 8)

Shenandoah National Park

	Miles from Front Royal, Va.			*Miles from Rockfish Gap, Va.*	
	32.9	Side trail to Jewell Hollow Overlook; Skyline Drive, mile 36.4	R	74.9	
	33.0	Pinnacles Picnic Ground; Skyline Drive, mile 36.7	Rw	74.8	
	35.2	Hughes River Gap; side trail to Stony Man Mountain Overlook; Skyline Drive, mile 38.6 (3,097')	Rw	72.6	
	36.8	Side trail to Stony Man summit		71.0	
	37.2	Skyland Service Road (north) (L,M 0.3m W)	RLM	70.6	
	38.0	Skyland Service Road (south)	R	69.8	
	40.1	Side trail to Crescent Rock Overlook; Skyline Drive, mile 44.4	R	67.7	
	40.5	Hawksbill Gap; Skyline Drive, mile 45.6 (3,361')	R	67.3	
	41.5	Side trail to Hawksbill Mountain, Byrd's Nest #2 Picnic Shelter (0.9m E)		66.3	
	41.8	Rock Spring Cabin (locked) & Hut (S,w 0.2m W)	Sw	66.0	
	43.7	Fishers Gap; Skyline Drive, mile 49.3	R	64.1	
	44.7	David Spring	w	63.1	
	45.3	Big Meadows (3,500') (C,L,M 0.1m E)	RCLM	62.5	
	46.2	Big Meadows Wayside, Harry F. Byrd, Sr., Visitor Center (w on A.T.; G,M 0.4m E)	RGMw	61.6	
	47.0	Spring	w	60.8	
	47.9	Milam Gap; Skyline Drive, mile 52.8	R	59.9	
	49.8	Hazeltop (3,812')		58.0	

Left margin labels: SNP Section 3 (Va. 8); SNP Section 4 (Va. 9); SNP Section 5 (Va. 10); Potomac A.T. Club

Right margin label: PATC Map 10

Shenandoah National Park

GBS	N to S	Features	Facilities (see page 8 for codes)	S to N	Map

Miles from Front Royal, Va. | | | *Miles from Rockfish Gap, Va.* |

	50.7	Bootens Gap; Skyline Drive, mile 55.1 (3,243')	R	57.1	
	53.3	Bearfence Mountain Hut (S,w 0.1m E)	Sw	54.5	
	54.0	Lewis Mountain Campground; Skyline Drive, mile 57.6 (C,G,L,w 0.1m W)	RCGLw	53.8	
	55.7	Spring	w	52.1	
	56.0	Pocosin Cabin (locked)	w	51.8	
	59.3	South River Picnic Grounds (w 0.1m W)	w	48.5	
	62.3	Swift Run Gap, U.S. 33; Skyline Drive, mile 65.5 (2,367')	R	45.5	
	63.6	Skyline Drive, mile 66.7	R	44.2	
	65.1	Hightop Mountain (3,587')		42.7	
	65.2	Spring	w	42.6	
	65.7	Hightop Hut (S 0.1m W; w 0.2m W)	Sw	42.1	
	66.9	Smith Roach Gap; Skyline Drive, mile 68.6	R	40.9	
	68.1	Little Roundtop Mountain		39.7	
	68.5	Powell Gap; Skyline Drive, mile 69.9 (2,294')	R	39.3	
	71.8	Simmons Gap; Skyline Drive, mile 73.2	Rw	36.0	
	73.7	Pinefield Gap; Skyline Drive, mile 75.2	R	34.1	
	73.9	Pinefield Hut	Sw	33.9	
	75.5	Ivy Creek Overlook; Skyline Drive, mile 77.5	R	32.3	
	77.6	Spring (w 0.1m W)	w	30.2	

SNP Section 5 (Va. 10) — SNP Section 6 (Va. 11) — SNP Section 7 (Va. 12)

PATC Map 10 — PATC Map 11 — Potomac A.T. Club

Shenandoah National Park

	N to S	Features	Facilities	S to N	
	Miles from Front Royal, Va.			*Miles from Rockfish Gap, Va.*	
	79.7	Loft Mountain Campground (3,300') (C,G,M,w 0.2m W)	CGMw	28.1	
	81.8	Doyles River Cabin (locked); Skyline Drive, mile 81.1 (w 0.3m E)	Rw	26.0	
	82.7	Doyles River Parking Overlook; Skyline Drive, mile 81.9	R	25.1	
	83.1	Skyline Drive, mile 82.2	R	24.7	
	84.0	Browns Gap; Skyline Drive, mile 82.9 (2,600')	R	23.8	
	85.5	Skyline Drive, mile 84.3	R	22.3	
	86.5	Blackrock (3,100')		21.3	
	87.1	Blackrock Hut (S,w 0.2m E)	Sw	20.7	
	87.6	Skyline Drive, mile 87.2	R	20.2	
	87.8	Blackrock Gap; Skyline Drive, mile 87.4 (2,321')	R	20.0	
	89.6	Skyline Drive, mile 88.9	R	18.2	
	93.7	Skyline Drive, mile 92.4 (3,100')	R	14.1	
	95.7	Turk Gap; Skyline Drive, mile 94.1	R	12.1	
	97.3	Skyline Drive, mile 95.3	R	10.5	
	98.9	Spring	w	8.9	
	99.1	Jarman Gap; Skyline Drive, mile 96.9; SNP southern boundary (2,173')	R	8.7	
	99.5	Spring	w	8.3	
	100.1	Calf Mountain Shelter (w 0.2m W; S 0.3m W)	Sw	7.7	
	102.3	Beagle Gap; Skyline Drive, mile 99.5	R	5.5	
	102.8	Bear Den Mountain (2,885')		5.0	
	104.1	McCormick Gap; Skyline Drive, mile 102.1	R	3.7	

Left margin labels: SNP Section 7 (Va. 12); SNP Section 8 (Va. 13); SNP Section 9 (Va. 14); Potomac A.T. Club

*Right margin label:* PATC Map 11

Shenandoah National Park

GBS	N to S	Features	Facilities (see page 8 for codes)	S to N	Map

Miles from
Front Royal, Va.

Miles from
Rockfish Gap, Va.

<table>
<tr><td rowspan="10" style="writing-mode:vertical">SNP Sec. 9 (Va.14)</td><td>107.0</td><td>Self-registration for SNP camping permits,
park entrance station
(0.2m W)</td><td></td><td>0.8</td><td rowspan="10" style="writing-mode:vertical">PATC Map 11   Potomac A.T. Club</td></tr>
<tr><td>107.5</td><td>Skyline Drive, mile 105.2</td><td>R</td><td>0.3</td></tr>
<tr><td>107.7</td><td>I-64 Overpass</td><td></td><td>0.1</td></tr>
<tr><td>107.8</td><td>Rockfish Gap, U.S. 250, I-64 (1,902');
Waynesboro, Va., P.O. 22980
(P.O.,G,L,M 4.5m W; G,L,M on A.T.)</td><td>☆
RGLM</td><td>0.0</td></tr>
</table>

Central Virginia

GBS	N to S	Features	Facilities (see page 8 for codes)	S to N	Map

Miles from Rockfish Gap, Va.

Miles from New River, Va.

0.0	Rockfish Gap, U.S. 250, I-64 (1,902'); **Waynesboro, Va., P.O. 22980** (P.O.,G,L,M 4.5m W; G,L,M on A.T.)	☆ RGLM	226.0
5.0	Mill Creek, Paul C. Wolfe Shelter	Sw	221.0
6.5	Side trail to Humpback Visitors Center (w 1.3m W)	w	219.5
6.8	Glass Hollow Overlook		219.2
9.0	Bear Spring	w	217.0
10.5	Side trail to Humpback Rocks		215.5
11.5	Humpback Mountain (3,600')		214.5
14.3	Dripping Rock Parking Area; Blue Ridge Parkway, mile 9.6	Rw	211.7
14.8	Cedar Cliffs		211.2
18.6	Three Ridges Parking Overlook; Blue Ridge Parkway, mile 13.1	R	207.4
19.1	Reids Gap, Va. 664; Blue Ridge Parkway, mile 13.6	R	206.9
20.8	Maupin Field Shelter	Sw	205.2
22.8	Hanging Rock		203.2
23.3	Three Ridges (3,870')		202.7
25.0	Chimney Rocks		201.0
27.0	Harpers Creek Shelter	Sw	199.0
29.7	Tye River	Cw	196.3
29.8	Va. 56 (970') (C,G 2.5m W)	RCG	196.2
31.1	Cripple Creek	w	194.9
34.1	The Priest (4,063')		191.9
34.6	The Priest Shelter	Sw	191.4

Old Dominion A.T. Club — Va. Section 15

Tidewater A.T. Club — Va. Section 16

Natural Bridge ATC — Va. Section 17

Central Va. Map 1

GBS	N to S	Features	Facilities (see page 8 for codes)	S to N	Map
	Miles from Rockfish Gap, Va.			*Miles from New River, Va.*	
	35.5	Crabtree Farm Road (Va. 826), Crabtree Falls Trail (C,w 0.5m W)	RCw	190.5	
	36.3	Cash Hollow Road (3,280')	R	189.7	
	37.6	Cash Hollow Rock		188.4	
	38.4	Spy Rock		187.6	
	38.9	Spy Rock Road (3,454'); **Montebello, Va., P.O. 24464** (P.O. 2.5m W; C,G,L,M 2.2m W)	RCGLM	187.1	
	40.1	Porters Field	Cw	185.9	
	41.2	Seeley-Woodworth Shelter	Sw	184.8	
	41.9	Elk Pond Branch	Cw	184.1	
	43.1	North Fork of Piney River	Cw	182.9	
	45.0	Greasy Spring Road	R	181.0	
	45.5	USFS 246	R	180.5	
	46.7	Salt Log Gap (north), USFS 63 (3,257')	R	179.3	
	48.0	Tar Jacket Ridge (3,847')		178.0	
	48.9	Hog Camp Gap, USFS 48 (3,485')	RCw	177.1	
	50.2	Cold Mountain (4,022')		175.8	
	51.4	Old Hotel Trail, Cow Camp Gap Shelter (3,428') (S,w 0.6m E)	Sw	174.6	
	52.4	Bald Knob (4,059')		173.6	
	55.2	U.S. 60 (2,065'); **Buena Vista, Va., P.O. 24416** (P.O.,C,G,L,M 9.3m W)	☆ RCGLM	170.8	
	57.0	Brown Mountain Creek Shelter	Sw	169.0	
	59.0	Pedlar Lake Road (USFS 38)	R	167.0	
	61.9	Pedlar River Bridge	w	164.1	
	62.0	USFS 39	R	164.0	

Va. 17 · Va. Section 18 · Va. Section 19 · Va. Section 20

Right margin (top to bottom): Central Va. Map 1 · Natural Bridge A.T. Club · Map 2

GBS	N to S	Features	Facilities (see page 8 for codes)	S to N	Map

Miles from Rockfish Gap, Va. — *Miles from New River, Va.*

	N to S	Features	Facilities	S to N
	63.9	Rice Mountain (2,228')		162.1
	65.8	Robinson Gap Road (Va. 607)	R	160.2
	66.1	Blue Ridge Parkway, mile 51.7; Punchbowl Mountain Crossing (2,170')	Rw	159.9
	66.5	Punchbowl Shelter (S,w 0.2m W)	Sw	159.5
	67.0	Punchbowl Mountain		159.0
	68.1	Bluff Mountain (3,372')		157.9
	69.6	Saltlog Gap (south) (2,573')		156.4
	70.7	Saddle Gap, Saddle Gap Trail		155.3
	72.2	Big Rocky Row (2,992')		153.8
	73.2	Fullers Rocks, Little Rocky Row (2,472')		152.8
	73.3	Rocky Row Trail		152.7
	75.3	Johns Hollow Shelter	Sw	150.7
	75.9	Va. 812 (USFS 36)	R	150.1
	76.0	Rocky Row Run (760')	Cw	150.0
	76.9	Lower Rocky Row Run bridge	w	149.1
	77.0	U.S. 501, Va. 130; **Big Island, Va., P.O. 24526; Glasgow, Va., P.O. 24555** (P.O.,G,M 5.6m E; P.O.,G,C,M 5.9m W; C,G,L 4.4m E)	☆ RCGLM	149.0
	77.2	James River Foot Bridge (678')		148.8
	78.4	Campsite	Cw	147.6
	79.2	Matts Creek Shelter	Sw	146.8
	81.1	Big Cove Branch	w	144.9
	81.9	Sulphur Spring Trail (north crossing) (2,588')		144.1
	82.4	Hickory Stand, Gunter Ridge Trail		143.6
	84.2	Sulphur Spring Trail (south crossing)		141.8

Natural Bridge A.T. Club

Va. Section 21

Va. Section 22

Central Va. Map 2

Central Virginia

	N to S	Features	Facilities (see page 8 for codes)	S to N	
	Miles from Rockfish Gap, Va.			*Miles from New River, Va.*	
	84.7	Marble Spring	Cw	141.3	
	85.7	Highcock Knob (3,073')		140.3	
	86.9	Petites Gap, USFS 35; Blue Ridge Parkway, mile 71.0 (2,369')	R	139.1	
	88.3	Harrison Ground Spring	w	137.7	
	90.2	Thunder Ridge Overlook; Blue Ridge Parkway, mile 74.7 (3,501')	R	135.8	
	90.6	Lower Blue Ridge Parkway crossing, mile 74.9	R	135.4	
	91.6	Thunder Hill Shelter	Sw	134.4	
	91.9	Upper Blue Ridge Parkway crossing, mile 76.3	R	134.1	
	92.5	The Guillotine		133.5	
	92.8	Apple Orchard Mountain (4,225')		133.2	
	94.2	Parkers Gap Road (USFS 812); Blue Ridge Parkway, mile 78.4 (3,430')	R	131.8	
	94.3	Apple Orchard Falls Trail		131.7	
	96.0	Black Rock		130.0	
	96.9	Cornelius Creek Shelter	Sw	129.1	
	97.5	Floyd Mountain (3,560')		128.5	
	101.8	Bryant Ridge Shelter (1,337')	Sw	124.2	
	104.0	Fork Mountain (2,042')		122.0	
	105.6	Va. 614, Jennings Creek (951') (w 0.3m E; C,G,L,M 1.6m E, L,M 4.5m W)	RCGLMw	120.4	
	107.1	Buchanan Trail		118.9	
	108.8	Cove Mountain Shelter	S(nw)	117.2	
	110.2	Little Cove Mountain Trail		115.8	
	110.6	Cove Mountain (2,720')		115.4	

*Left margin:* Va. Section 23 — Va. Section 24 — Va. Section 25

Right margin: Central Va. Map 2 — Natural Bridge A.T. Club

Central Virginia

Miles from Rockfish Gap, Va.

Miles from New River, Va.

	N to S	Features	Facilities	S to N	
	112.2	Bearwallow Gap, Va. 43, Blue Ridge Parkway, mile 90.9 (2,228'); **Buchanan, Va., P.O. 24066** (P.O.,G,M 5m W; L,M 7m W; C,L,M 4.9m E)	RCGLM	113.8	
	113.9	Blue Ridge Parkway, mile 91.8; Mills Gap Overlook	R	112.1	
	114.6	Blue Ridge Parkway, mile 92.5; Peaks of Otter Overlook	R	111.4	
	115.3	Bobblets Gap Shelter (S,w 0.2m W)	Sw	110.7	
	117.7	Blue Ridge Parkway, mile 95.3; Harveys Knob Overlook	R	108.3	
	118.3	Blue Ridge Parkway, mile 95.9; Montvale Overlook	R	107.7	
	119.4	Blue Ridge Parkway, mile 97.0; Taylors Mountain Overlook	R	106.6	
	120.2	Black Horse Gap, Old Fincastle Road (USFS 186); Blue Ridge Parkway, mile 97.7 (2,402')	R	105.8	
	122.2	Spring	w	103.8	
	122.6	Wilson Creek Shelter	Sw	103.4	
	123.3	Wilson Creek	w	102.7	
	125.2	Curry Creek	w	100.8	
	126.0	Salt Pond Road (USFS 191)	R	100.0	
	128.8	Fullhardt Knob Shelter (2,676')	Sw	97.2	
	131.8	Va. 652	R	94.2	

Left margin (top to bottom): *Natural Bridge A.T. Club* — Va. Section 26; *Roanoke A.T. Club* — Va. Section 27

Right margin: Central Va. Map 2; Central Va. Map 3

Central Virginia

*Miles from
Rockfish Gap, Va.*

*Miles from
New River, Va.*

	N to S	Features	Facilities	S to N
Va. Section 27	132.3	Norfolk Southern Railway, U.S. 11; **Troutville, Va., P.O. 24175** (P.O.,G 0.8m W)	☆ RG	93.7
	132.6	Va. 779, I-81	R	93.4
	133.8	U.S. 220; **Daleville, Va., P.O. 24083; Cloverdale, Va., P.O. 24077** (P.O. 1m W; P.O.,G,L,M 2.3m E; G,L,M on A.T.)	RGLM	92.2
	134.3	Tinker Creek (1,165')		91.7
	137.8	Hay Rock, Tinker Ridge		88.2
	138.9	Angels Gap		87.1
Va. Section 28	142.9	Lamberts Meadow Campsite, Sawmill Run	Cw	83.1
	143.2	Lamberts Meadow Shelter	Sw	82.8
	143.8	Scorched Earth Gap, Andy Layne Trail		82.2
	144.3	Tinker Cliffs (3,000')		81.7
	146.1	Brickey's Gap		79.9
	149.2	Campbell Shelter	Sw	76.8
	149.3	Pig Farm Campsite	Cw	76.7
	149.9	McAfee Knob (3,197')		76.1
	151.6	Catawba Mountain Shelter	Sw	74.4
	152.6	Johns Spring Shelter	S	73.4
	153.6	Va. 311; **Catawba, Va., P.O. 24070** (P.O.,G 1m W; L 1.7m W; M 1.3m W)	RGLM	72.4
	157.9	Va. 785 (1,790') (L 0.9m E)	RL	68.1

Central Va. Map 3

Roanoke A.T. Club

Central Virginia

Roanoke A.T. Club (RATC)

GBS	N to S	Features	Facilities (see page 8 for codes)	S to N	Map

Miles from Rockfish Gap, Va.

Miles from New River, Va.

	N to S	Features	Facilities	S to N	
	159.5	Va. 624, North Mountain Trail (G,L 0.4m W)	RGL	66.5	
	160.5	Rawies Rest		65.5	
Va. Section 29	161.0	Lost Spectacles Gap		65.0	Central Va. Map 3
	162.0	Dragons Tooth, Cove Mountain (3,020')		64.0	
	166.2	Pickle Branch Shelter (S,w 0.3m E)	Sw	59.8	
	167.4	Trout Creek, Va. 620 (1,525')	R	58.6	
	171.2	Audie Murphy Monument (3,100')		54.8	
	175.0	Craig Creek Valley, Va. 621 (1,540')	R	51.0	
Va. Section 30	176.3	Niday Shelter	Sw	49.7	
	177.0	Cabin Branch	Cw	49.0	
	178.7	Sinking Creek Mountain (3,450')		47.3	
	182.3	Sarver Hollow Shelter (S,w 0.4m E)	Sw	43.7	Central Va. Map 4
	185.4	Va. 630, Sinking Creek (2,100')	Rw	40.6	
	186.3	Sinking Creek Valley, Va. 42	R	39.7	
Va. Section 31	187.7	Spring	w	38.3	
	188.7	Laurel Creek Shelter	Sw	37.3	
	191.7	Rocky Gap, Va. 601	R	34.3	
	192.7	Stream	w	33.3	
	193.7	Johns Creek Valley, USFS 156 (2,080')	Rw	32.3	
	194.5	War Spur Shelter	Sw	31.5	
	198.2	Campsites, spring	Cw	27.8	
Va. Section 32	199.4	Wind Rock (4,100')		26.6	
	199.6	Mountain Lake Road/ Salt Sulphur Turnpike (Va. 613)	R	26.4	
	203.3	Bailey Gap Shelter	S	22.7	
	203.5	Spring	w	22.5	
	204.8	Va. 635, Stony Creek (2,450')	R	21.2	

Central Virginia

GBS	N to S	Features	Facilities (see page 8 for codes)	S to N	Map

*Miles from
Rockfish Gap, Va.*

*Miles from
New River, Va.*

	205.8	Dismal Branch	w	20.2	
	206.9	Va. 635, Stony Creek Valley	R	19.1	
	207.2	Pine Swamp Branch Shelter	Sw	18.8	
	209.7	Allegheny Trail		16.3	
	209.9	Peters Mountain (3,860')		16.1	
	212.0	Dickenson Gap		14.0	
	213.6	Groundhog Trail		12.4	
	214.6	Symms Gap Meadow		11.4	
	218.1	Campsite, water	Cw	7.9	
	219.7	Rice Field Shelter (3,400') (S on A.T.; w 0.5m E)	Sw	6.3	
	222.3	Springs	Cw	3.7	
	224.5	Clendennin Road (Va. 641)	R	1.5	
	226.0	U.S. 460, Senator Shumate Bridge (east end), New River (1,600') (G 0.1m E)	RG	0.0	

Va. Section 33

RATC

Central Va. Map 4

Outdoor Club of Va. Tech

GBS	N to S	Features	Facilities (see page 8 for codes)	S to N	Map

Miles from New River, Va.   *Miles from Damascus, Va.*

	N to S	Features	Facilities	S to N	
	0.0	U.S. 460, Senator Shumate Bridge (east end), New River (1,600') (G 0.1m E)	RG	164.4	
	0.5	Lane Street, **Pearisburg, Va., P.O. 24134** ☆ (P.O.,G,L,M 1m E; L 0.2m E)	RGLM	163.9	
	1.0	Va. 634	R	163.4	
	1.4	Spring	w	163.0	
	3.0	Angels Rest, Pearis Mountain (3,550')		161.4	
	3.5	Campsite, spring	Cw	160.9	
	8.7	Doc's Knob Shelter	Sw	155.7	
	10.9	Sugar Run Gap, Sugar Run Gap Road (Va. 663)	R	153.5	
	12.5	Big Horse Gap, USFS 103 (3,800')	R	151.9	
	12.6	Ribble Trail, north junction	w	151.8	
	18.1	Wapiti Shelter (2,600')	Sw	146.3	
	19.6	Stream	w	144.8	
	20.0	Ribble Trail, south junction; White Cedar Horse Campground (C,w 1.5m W)	Cw	144.4	
	23.9	Dismal Creek Falls Trail		140.5	
	25.8	Va. 606 (2,100') (C,G,M,w 0.8m W)	RCGMw	138.6	
	25.9	Kimberling Creek		138.5	
	27.8	Brushy Mountain (2,900')		136.6	
	31.1	Va. 608, Lickskillet Hollow (2,200')	R	133.3	
	32.3	Jenny Knob Shelter	Sw	132.1	
	34.0	Brushy Mountain (3,101')		130.4	
	35.4	Va. 611	R	129.0	
	42.1	Helveys Mill Shelter (S,w 0.3m E)	Sw	122.3	
	43.6	Va. 612, Kimberling Creek	Rw	120.8	

Left margin (top to bottom): Roanoke A.T. Club — Va. Section 34 — Va. 35 — Va. Section 36 — OCVT

*Right margin:* SW Va. Map 1 — Map 2

Southwest Virginia

GBS	N to S	Features	Facilities (see page 8 for codes)	S to N	Map

Miles from New River, Va.

Miles from Damascus, Va.

	N to S	Features	Facilities	S to N	
	44.2	I-77 Crossing	R	120.2	
	44.4	U.S. 52 (2,920'); **Bastian, Va., P.O. 24314; Bland, Va., P.O. 24315**	☆		
		(P.O. 1.8m W; P.O.,G,L,M 2.5m E)	RGLM	120.0	
	51.3	Va. 615, Laurel Creek (2,450')	RCw	113.1	
	51.9	Brushy Mountain (3,080')		112.5	
	56.1	Jenkins Shelter (2,470')	Sw	108.3	
	59.1	Davis Farm Campsite (C,w 0.5m W)	Cw	105.3	
	59.9	Va. 623, Garden Mountain (3,880')	R	104.5	
	64.6	Spring (w 0.2m E)	w	99.8	
	64.8	Walker Gap (3,520')	Rw	99.6	
	66.1	Chestnut Knob Shelter (4,409')	S(nw)	98.3	
	67.9	Spring-fed pond	w	96.5	
	70.7	USFS 222 (2,300')	R	93.7	
	72.0	Lick Creek	w	92.4	
	74.0	Lynn Camp Creek (2,400')	w	90.4	
	75.0	Campsite, spring	Cw	89.4	
	75.2	Knot Maul Branch Shelter	S (nw)	89.2	
	76.5	Brushy Mountain (3,200')		87.9	
	77.3	Va. 42; **Ceres, Va., P.O. 24318** (P.O. 5.2m E; w 0.2m E)	Rw	87.1	
	78.3	Va. 742, North Fork of Holston River		86.1	
	79.7	Va. 610	R	84.7	
	81.1	Tilson Gap, Big Walker Mountain (3,500')		83.3	
	82.8	Crawfish Valley (2,600') (w on A.T.; C,w 0.3m E)	Cw	81.6	
	83.9	Gullion (Little Brushy) Mountain (3,300')		80.5	

*Left margin:* Va. Section 37 · Va. Section 38 · Va. Section 39

Right margin: OCVT · Piedmont A.T. Hikers · SW Va. Map 2 · SW Va. Map 3

Southwest Virginia

	N to S	Features	Facilities	S to N	
	Miles from New River, Va.			*Miles from Damascus, Va.*	
Va. 39	86.4	Davis Path Campsite	C(nw)	78.0	
	87.3	Spring	w	77.1	
	88.0	Va. 617	R	76.4	
	89.1	Va. 683, U.S. 11, I-81 (2,420'); **Atkins, Va., P.O. 24311** (P.O.,G,M 3.2m W; G,L,M on A.T.)	RGLM	75.3	
Va. Section 40	91.3	Va. 729	R	73.1	
	91.8	Va. 615	R	72.6	
	93.3	USFS 644	R	71.1	
	93.6	Chatfield Shelter	Sw	70.8	
	95.6	Glade Mountain (3,900')		68.8	
	96.5	USFS 86	Cw	67.9	SW Va. Map 3
	96.9	Locust Mountain		67.5	
	99.4	Brushy Mountain		65.0	
	99.9	Va. 622	R	64.5	
	100.6	Va. 16 (3,220'); **Sugar Grove, Va., P.O. 24375** (P.O.,G 3.2m E; G 3m W)	RGw	63.8	
Va. Section 41	100.7	Partnership Shelter	Sw	63.7	
	104.7	Va. 601	R	59.7	
	107.5	Teas Road	R	56.9	
	108.5	Va. 670, South Fork Holston River (2,450')	R	55.9	
	109.8	Va. 672	R	54.6	
	111.3	Trimpi Shelter	Sw	53.1	
	113.1	High Point (4,040')		51.3	
	113.7	Campsite, Spring (C,w 0.2m E)	Cw	50.7	

Mt. Rogers A.T. Club — Piedmont A.T. Hikers

Southwest Virginia

	Miles from New River, Va.		*Miles from Damascus, Va.*	
	115.2	Dickey Gap, Va. 16, Va. 650; **Troutdale, Va., P.O. 24378** (P.O. 2.6m E; L 3.8m E)	RGLM	49.2
	116.4	Comers Creek, Comers Creek Falls Trail (3,100')w		48.0
	117.3	Dickey Gap Trail (C,w 0.5m W)	Cw	47.1
	119.0	Stream	w	45.4
	119.8	Hurricane Creek Trail		44.6
	120.4	Hurricane Mountain Shelter	Sw	44.0
	121.4	Chestnut Flats, Iron Mountain Trail, Tennessee-New River Divide		43.0
	121.7	Hurricane Mountain (4,320')		42.7
	123.7	Va. 603, Fox Creek (3,480') (C,w on A.T., 2m W)	RCw	40.7
	125.4	Old Orchard Shelter	Sw	39.0
	127.1	Pine Mountain (5,000')		37.3
	128.5	The Scales		35.9
	128.8	Stone Mountain		35.6
	130.0	Spring	w	34.4
	131.0	Big Wilson Creek	Cw	33.4
	131.3	Grayson Highlands State Park, Wise Shelter (4,460') (S,w on A.T.; C,w 2m E)	CSw	33.1
	133.5	Park service road to Massie Gap		30.9
	134.3	Wilburn Ridge		30.1
	135.6	Rhododendron Gap (5,440')		28.8
	136.4	Thomas Knob Shelter	Sw	28.0
	136.8	Mt. Rogers Spur Trail		27.6
	138.6	Deep Gap (w 0.2m E)	w	25.8

Va. Section 42

Va. Section 43

SW Va. Map 3

SW Va. Map 4

Mt. Rogers A.T. Club

Southwest Virginia

GBS	N to S	Features	Facilities (see page 8 for codes)	S to N	Map
	Miles from New River, Va.			*Miles from Damascus, Va.*	
	140.6	Va. 600, Elk Garden (4,434')	R	23.8	
	143.1	Whitetop Mountain Road (USFS 89)	RCw	21.3	
	143.3	Spring	w	21.1	
	143.8	Buzzard Rock, Whitetop Mountain (5,080')		20.6	
	146.3	Va. 601 (Beech Mountain Road)	Rw	18.1	
	147.2	Campsites, streams	Cw	17.2	
	147.5	U.S. 58 (3,160'); Summit Cut, Va.	R	16.9	
	148.6	Lost Mountain Shelter	Sw	15.8	
	149.6	Spring	w	14.8	
	149.8	Va. 859 (Grassy Ridge Road)	R	14.6	
	150.4	Virginia Creeper Trail, Whitetop Laurel Creek		14.0	
	150.8	Va. 728, Creek Junction (2,720')	R	13.6	
	152.6	Campsite	Cw	11.8	
	152.7	Bear Tree Gap side trail (C 0.6m W)	C	11.7	
	155.0	Saunders Shelter (S,w 0.2m W)	Sw	9.4	
	155.3	Straight Mountain (3,500')		9.1	
	156.8	Taylors Valley Side Trail		7.6	
	157.5	Stream	w	6.9	
	158.8	U.S. 58, Straight Branch, Feathercamp Branch (2,200'), Feathercamp Trail	Rw	5.6	
	159.5	Beech Grove Trail		4.9	
	160.9	Feathercamp Ridge, Iron Mountain Trail (2,850')		3.5	
	163.3	U.S. 58, Va. 91, Virginia Creeper Trail	R	1.1	
	164.4	**Damascus, Va., P.O. 24236 (1,928')**	☆		
		(P.O.,G,L,M on A.T.)	RGLM	0.0	

Va. Section 44

Va. Section 45

Mt. Rogers A.T. Club

SW Va. Map 4

Miles from Damascus, Va.

Miles from Fontana Dam, N.C.

N to S	Features	Facilities	S to N
0.0	**Damascus, Va., P.O. 24236** (1,928')	☆	
	(P.O.,G,L,M on A.T.)	RGLM	300.9
2.1	Spring	w	298.8
3.7	Virginia–Tennessee Line		297.2
10.2	Abingdon Gap Shelter (3,785')	Sw	290.7
11.3	McQueens Gap, USFS 69	R	289.6
11.7	McQueens Knob		289.2
13.1	Double Spring Gap	w	287.8
15.0	Low Gap, U.S. 421 (3,384');		
	Shady Valley, Tenn., P.O. 37688		
	(w on A.T.; P.O.,G,M 3m E)	RGMw	285.9
18.5	Double Springs Shelter,		
	Holston Mountain Trail (4,080')	Sw	282.4
19.4	Campsite	w	281.5
21.5	Tenn. 91 (3,450')	R	279.4
22.3	Stream	w	278.6
24.7	Spring	w	276.2
24.8	Nick Grindstaff Monument		276.1
26.1	Iron Mountain Shelter (4,125')	S(nw)	274.8
26.3	Spring	w	274.6
27.7	Turkeypen Gap		273.2
29.1	Spring	w	271.8
32.9	Vandeventer Shelter (3,510')		
	(S on A.T.; w 0.5m W)	Sw	268.0
34.6	Spring	w	266.3
37.6	Wilbur Dam Road	R	263.3
38.9	Watauga Dam (north end)		262.0
40.1	Watauga Lake Shelter (2,100')	Sw	260.8
40.4	Griffith Branch	Cw	260.5

Tenn.–N.C. Section 1

Tenn.–N.C. Section 2

Tenn.–N.C. Section 3

Tenn.–N.C. Map 1

Tennessee Eastman Hiking Club   MRATC

Tennessee–North Carolina

GBS	N to S	Features	Facilities (see page 8 for codes)	S to N	Map
	Miles from Damascus, Va.			*Miles from Fontana Dam, N.C.*	
	41.8	U.S. 321; **Hampton, Tenn., P.O. 37658** (P.O.,G,M 2.6m W; G,L 1.8m W)	RCGLM	259.1	
	44.9	Pond Flats	Cw	256.0	
	47.7	Side trail to U.S. 321	w	253.2	
	48.2	Waycaster Spring	w	252.7	
	48.5	Laurel Fork Shelter (2,400')	Sw	252.4	
	49.2	Laurel Fork Falls	w	251.7	
	50.4	Dennis Cove, USFS 50 (C,G,L,M 0.5m E; C,L 0.2m W)	RCGLMw	250.5	
	52.1	Trail to Coon Den Falls		248.8	
	54.6	Campsite	Cw	246.3	
	55.4	White Rocks Mountain (4,206')		245.5	
	56.7	Moreland Gap Shelter	Sw	244.2	
	58.6	Campsite	Cw	242.3	
	62.5	Upper Laurel Fork		238.4	
	63.5	Stream		237.4	
	64.7	Walnut Mountain Road	R	236.2	
	65.5	Campsite	Cw	235.4	
	66.3	Mountaineer Shelter	Sw	234.6	
	66.5	Campsite	Cw	234.4	
	68.7	Campsite	Cw	232.2	
	71.5	Campbell Hollow Road	R	229.4	
	71.8	Buck Mountain Road	R	229.1	
	74.9	Bear Branch Road	R	226.0	
	75.1	U.S. 19E (2,895'); **Roan Mountain, Tenn., P.O. 37687; Elk Park, N.C., P.O. 28622** (P.O.,G,M 3.4m W; P.O. 2.5m E; C 4.0m E; G 1.2m E; L 3m E; M 0.5m E, 1m E)	RCGLM	225.8	

Left margin labels: *Tennessee Eastman Hiking Club*; Tenn.–N.C. Section 5; Tenn.–N.C. 4

Right margin labels: Tenn.–N.C. Map 1; Tenn.–N.C. Map 2

Tennessee–North Carolina

GBS	N to S	Features	Facilities (see page 8 for codes)	S to N	Map

Miles from Damascus, Va.

Miles from Fontana Dam, N.C.

	N to S	Features	Facilities	S to N	
	75.7	Spring	w	225.2	
	78.1	Doll Flats	Cw	222.8	
Tenn.–N.C. Section 6	80.5	Hump Mountain (5,587')		220.4	
	81.4	Bradley Gap	Cw	219.5	
	82.7	Little Hump Mountain (5,459')	C	218.2	
	84.3	Yellow Mountain Gap, Overmountain Shelter (4,682') (C on A.T.; w 0.2m E; S 0.3m E)	CSw	216.6	
	86.2	Stan Murray Shelter (5,050')	Sw	214.7	
	88.0	Side trail to Grassy Ridge		212.9	
Tenn.–N.C. 7	89.9	Carvers Gap, Tenn. 143, N.C. 261 (5,512')	Rw	211.0	Tennessee Eastman Hiking Club
	91.4	Roan High Knob Shelter (6,285')	Sw	209.5	
	93.2	Ash Gap	Cw	207.7	Tenn.–N.C. Map 2
Tenn.–N.C. Section 8	96.2	Hughes Gap (4,040') (G 3.2m W; C,L 2m E)	RCGL	204.7	
	98.4	Little Rock Knob (4,918')		202.5	
	99.3	Clyde Smith Shelter	Sw	201.6	
	100.4	Campsite	Cw	200.5	
	101.2	Greasy Creek Gap (4,034') (C,w 0.2m W; L 0.7m E)	CLw	199.7	
	104.0	Campsite	Cw	196.9	
Tenn.–N.C. 9	105.3	Iron Mountain Gap, Tenn. 107, N.C. 226 (3,723') (G 4.7m W)	RG	195.6	
	108.4	Cherry Gap Shelter	Sw	192.5	
	109.5	Low Gap (3,900')	w	191.4	
	111.7	Unaka Mountain (5,180')		189.2	
	112.7	USFS 230	R	188.2	
	113.3	Deep Gap (4,100')	Cw	187.6	

Tennessee–North Carolina

GBS	N to S	Features	Facilities (see page 8 for codes)	S to N	Map
	Miles from Damascus, Va.		*Miles from Fontana Dam, N.C.*		
	114.3	Beauty Spot Gap	Rw	186.6	
	114.8	Beauty Spot		186.1	
	116.0	USFS 230	R	184.9	
	117.1	Indian Grave Gap (C 3.3m W)	RC	183.8	
	121.2	Curley Maple Gap Shelter (3,070')	Sw	179.7	
	124.1	Nolichucky River Valley (C,L,M on A.T.)	RCLM	176.8	
	125.4	Nolichucky River (1,700'); **Erwin, Tenn., P.O. 37650** (P.O.,G,M 3.8m W; L 1.2m W; G,L 2.3m W)	☆ RGLM	175.5	
	129.3	Temple Hill Gap (2,850')		171.6	
	131.7	No Business Knob Shelter	S	169.2	
	131.9	Spring	w	169.0	
	136.0	Oglesby Branch	w	164.9	
	136.6	Spivey Gap, U.S. 19W (3,200')	Rw	164.3	
	137.1	Campsite	Cw	163.8	
	138.6	Trail to High Rocks (4,100')		162.3	
	138.9	Whistling Gap	C	162.0	
	140.9	Little Bald		160.0	
	141.9	Campsite	Cw	159.0	
	142.3	Bald Mountain Shelter	Sw	158.6	
	143.2	Big Stamp (C,w 0.3m W; M 1.5m E)	CMw	157.7	
	143.5	Big Bald (5,516')		157.4	
	144.3	Spring	w	156.6	
	146.3	Low Gap	Cw	154.6	
	147.7	Street Gap (4,100')		153.2	
	149.3	Springs	w	151.6	

Left margin labels: Tenn.–N.C. Section 9 · Tenn.–N.C. Section 10 · Tenn.–N.C. Section 11 · Tennessee Eastman Hiking Club · Carolina Mountain Club

Right margin labels: Map 2 · Tenn.–N.C. Map 3

Tennessee–North Carolina

GBS	N to S	Features	Facilities (see page 8 for codes)	S to N	Map

Miles from Damascus, Va.

Miles from Fontana Dam, N.C.

	150.0	Sams Gap, U.S. 23, I-26 (3,800')			
		(M 1.9m E, 2.8m E; G 3.2m E)	RGM	150.9	
	151.8	High Rock (4,460')		149.1	
	152.4	Hogback Ridge Shelter			
		(S 0.1m E; w 0.3m E)	Sw	148.5	
	153.6	Rice Gap (3,800')		147.3	
	154.6	Big Flat	C	146.3	
	155.2	Frozen Knob (4,579')		145.7	
	158.0	Rector Laurel Road (2,960')	R	142.9	
	158.5	Devil Fork Gap, N.C. 212	R	142.4	
	160.3	Campsite	Cw	140.6	
	161.2	Flint Mountain Shelter (3,550')	Sw	139.7	
	163.9	Spring	w	137.0	
	165.2	Big Butt (4,750')	C	135.7	
	167.1	Jerry Cabin Shelter (4,150')	Sw	133.8	
	169.6	Big Firescald Knob	w	131.3	
	170.6	Blackstack Cliffs (0.1m W)		130.3	
	170.8	White Rock Cliffs (0.1m E)		130.1	
	170.9	Spring	w	130.0	
	172.6	Camp Creek Bald,			
		side trail to fire tower (4,750')	R	128.3	
	173.9	Little Laurel Shelter (3,300')	Sw	127.0	
	177.2	Log Cabin Drive	R	123.7	
	178.8	Allen Gap, N.C. 208, Tenn. 70 (2,234')	Rw	122.1	
	181.0	Spring	w	119.9	
	182.5	Spring Mountain Shelter (3,300')	Sw	118.4	
	184.2	Hurricane Gap	R	116.7	
	185.3	Rich Mountain Fire Tower			
		Side Trail (3,600')	Cw	115.6	
	187.6	Tanyard Gap, U.S. 25 & 70 (2,278')	R	113.3	

Left margin: Tenn.–N.C. Section 12 · Tenn.–N.C. Section 13 · Tenn.–N.C. Sec. 14

Right margin: Tenn.–N.C. Map 3 · Tenn.–N.C. Map 4 · Carolina Mountain Club

Tennessee–North Carolina

GBS	N to S	Features	Facilities (see page 8 for codes)	S to N	Map
		Miles from Damascus, Va.	*Miles from Fontana Dam, N.C.*		
Sec. 14	188.6	Campsite	C	112.3	
	190.2	Pump Gap		110.7	
	192.1	Lovers Leap Rock		108.8	
	193.5	U.S. 25 & 70, N.C. 209 (1,326'); **Hot Springs, N.C., P.O. 28743** (P.O.,C,G,L,M on A.T.)	☆ RCGLM	107.4	
Tenn.–N.C. Section 15	196.7	Deer Park Mountain Shelter	Sw	104.2	
	200.1	Garenflo Gap (2,500')	R	100.8	
	202.6	Big Rock Spring	w	98.3	
	204.2	Bluff Mountain (4,686')		96.7	
	206.6	Walnut Mountain Shelter	Sw	94.3	
	207.9	Lemon Gap, N.C. 1182, Tenn. 107 (3,550')	R	93.0	Tenn.–N.C. Map 4
	211.5	Roaring Fork Shelter	Sw	89.4	
	213.3	Max Patch Summit (4,629')		87.6	
	214.1	Max Patch Road (N.C. 1182)	R	86.8	
	216.8	Brown Gap	RCw	84.1	
	219.7	Deep Gap, Groundhog Creek Shelter (2,900') (S,w 0.2m E)	Sw	81.2	
Tenn.–N.C. Section 16	221.7	Campsite	Cw	79.2	
	222.2	Snowbird Mountain (4,263')	R	78.7	
	223.7	Spanish Oak Gap		77.2	
	224.6	Painter Branch	Cw	76.3	
	226.9	Green Corner Road (C,G,L 0.2m W)	RCGL	74.0	
	227.4	I-40	R	73.5	
	227.8	Pigeon River (1,400')		73.1	
	228.0	State Line Branch	Cw	72.9	

Carolina Mountain Club

Tennessee–North Carolina

GBS	N to S	Features	Facilities (see page 8 for codes)	S to N	Map

Miles from Damascus, Va.

Miles from Fontana Dam, N.C.

	N to S	Features	Facilities	S to N	
	229.3	Davenport Gap, Tenn. 32, N.C. 284; eastern boundary, Great Smoky Mountains National Park (1,975') (C 2.5m E)	RC	71.6	
	230.2	Davenport Gap Shelter	Sw	70.7	
	232.4	Spring	w	68.5	
	234.0	Spring	w	66.9	
	234.5	Mt. Cammerer Side Trail (5,000')		66.4	
	236.6	Low Gap Trail		64.3	
	237.3	Cosby Knob Shelter	Sw	63.6	
	237.9	Cosby Knob		63.0	
	241.2	Snake Den Ridge Trail		59.7	
	243.1	Mt. Guyot Side Trail		57.8	
	243.2	Guyot Spring	w	57.7	
	243.8	Guyot Spur (6,360')		57.1	
	245.0	Tri-Corner Knob Shelter	Sw	55.9	
	246.0	Mt. Chapman		54.9	
	247.5	Mt. Sequoyah		53.4	
	250.2	Pecks Corner Shelter (w on A.T.; S,w 0.5m E)	Sw	50.7	
	251.5	Bradleys View		49.4	
	254.8	Porters Gap, the Sawteeth		46.1	
	256.7	Charlies Bunion		44.2	
	257.6	Icewater Spring Shelter	Sw	43.3	
	257.9	Boulevard Trail to Mt. LeConte		43.0	
	260.6	Newfound Gap, U.S. 441 (5,045')	Rw	40.3	
	262.3	Indian Gap	R	38.6	
	265.1	Mt. Collins Shelter (5,900') (S,w 0.5m W)	Sw	35.8	
	267.3	Mt. Love		33.6	

Left margin: Tenn.–N.C. Section 17 (N.C. 1) · Sec. 18 (N.C. 2)

Right margin: Smoky Mountains Hiking Club · Great Smoky Mtns. N.P. Map

Tennessee–North Carolina

GBS	N to S	Features	Facilities (see page 8 for codes)	S to N	Map

*Miles from
Damascus, Va.*

*Miles from
Fontana Dam, N.C.*

	N to S	Features	Facilities	S to N	
	268.5	Clingmans Dome (6,643')			
		(R,w 0.5m E)	Rw	32.4	
	271.4	Double Spring Gap Shelter (5,507')	Sw	29.5	
	272.9	Silers Bald		28.0	
	273.1	Silers Bald Shelter	Sw	27.8	
	275.8	Buckeye Gap (4,817')	w	25.1	
	278.4	Sams Gap	w	22.5	
	278.6	Derrick Knob Shelter	Sw	22.3	
	279.7	Sugar Tree Gap (4,435')		21.2	
	282.1	Mineral Gap (5,030')		18.8	
	282.8	Beechnut Gap	w	18.1	
	283.1	Thunderhead, east peak (5,527')		17.8	
	283.7	Rocky Top		17.2	
	284.9	Eagle Creek Trail to Spence Field Shelter, Bote Mountain Trail			
		(S,w 0.2m E)	Sw	16.0	
	287.8	Russell Field Shelter	Sw	13.1	
	288.6	Little Abrams Gap (4,120')		12.3	
	290.0	Devils Tater Patch (4,775')		10.9	
	290.6	Mollies Ridge Shelter	Sw	10.3	
	292.0	Ekaneetlee Gap (3,842')	w	8.9	
	293.4	Doe Knob (4,520')		7.5	
	295.7	Birch Spring Gap	Cw	5.2	
	296.9	Shuckstack fire tower (0.1m E)		4.0	
	300.9	Little Tennessee River, Fontana Dam; southern boundary, Great Smoky Mountains National Park (1,800')	R	0.0	

Smoky Mountains Hiking Club

Tenn.–N.C. Section 18 (N.C. 2)

Great Smoky Mtns. N.P. Map

GBS	N to S	Features	Facilities (see page 8 for codes)	S to N	Map

Miles from Fontana Dam, N.C.   *Miles from Springer Mountain, Ga.*

	N to S	Features	Facilities	S to N	
	0.0	Little Tennessee River, Fontana Dam; southern boundary, Great Smoky Mountains National Park (1,781')	R	166.5	
	0.4	Fontana Dam Visitors Center	Rw	166.1	
	0.7	Fontana Dam Shelter	Sw	165.8	
	1.8	N.C. 28; **Fontana Dam, N.C., P.O. 28733** (P.O.,G,L,M 1.8m W)	RGLM	164.7	
	4.1	Campsite	Cw	162.4	
	4.5	Walker Gap (3,450')		162.0	
	5.9	Black Gum Gap		160.6	
	7.3	Cable Gap Shelter	Sw	159.2	
	8.2	Yellow Creek Gap, S.R. 1242 (2,980') (Yellow Creek Mountain Road) (L 4m E)	RL	158.3	
	10.6	Cody Gap	Cw	155.9	
	11.4	Hogback Gap		155.1	
	13.2	Brown Fork Gap	w	153.3	
	13.4	Brown Fork Gap Shelter	Sw	153.1	
	14.8	Sweetwater Gap		151.7	
	15.8	Stecoah Gap, N.C. 143 (3,165') (Sweetwater Creek Road)	Rw	150.7	
	17.9	Simp Gap		148.6	
	18.9	Locust Cove Gap	Cw	147.6	
	21.3	Cheoah Bald (5,062')		145.2	
	22.5	Sassafras Gap Shelter	Sw	144.0	
	23.4	Swim Bald		143.1	
	26.3	Grassy Gap (3,050')		140.2	
	27.8	Wright Gap	R	138.7	

N.C. Section 3   N.C. Section 4   N.C. Section 5

N.C.–Ga. Map 1

Smoky Mountains Hiking Club

North Carolina–Georgia

			Facilities (see page 8 for codes)		

Miles from Fontana Dam, N.C. | *Miles from Springer Mountain, Ga.*

29.4	U.S. 19, U.S. 74, Nantahala River (1,723'); Wesser, N.C. (L,M on A.T.; G 1m E)	RGLM	137.1
30.2	A. Rufus Morgan Shelter	Sw	136.3
33.5	Jump-up Lookout (4,000')		133.0
35.1	Wesser Creek Trail, Wesser Bald Shelter	CS	131.4
35.2	Spring	w	131.3
35.9	Wesser Bald (4,627'), viewing tower (0.1m E)		130.6
37.3	Tellico Gap, S.R. 1365 (3,850')	R	129.2
38.7	Spring	w	127.8
39.0	Side trail to Rocky Bald Lookout		127.5
40.2	Copper Ridge Bald Lookout (5,080')		126.3
40.9	Cold Spring Shelter	CSw	125.6
42.1	Burningtown Gap, S.R. 1397 (4,236')	R	124.4
44.4	Licklog Gap (w 0.5m W)	w	122.1
45.7	Wayah Shelter	CSw	120.8
46.2	Campsite	Cw	120.3
46.6	Wayah Bald (5,342')	R	119.9
48.5	Wine Spring	Cw	118.0
49.0	USFS 69	Rw	117.5
50.8	Wayah Gap, S.R. 1310 (4,180')	R	115.7
52.5	Siler Bald Shelter (4,700') (S,w 0.5m E)	Sw	114.0
54.7	Panther Gap		111.8
55.6	Swinging Lick Gap		110.9
55.8	Campsite	Cw	110.7

Left margin: *Nantahala Hiking Club* — N.C. Section 6 — N.C. Section 7 — N.C. Section 8

Right margin: N.C.–Ga. Map 2

North Carolina–Georgia

GBS	N to S	Features	Facilities (see page 8 for codes)	S to N	Map

Miles from Fontana Dam, N.C.

Miles from Springer Mountain, Ga.

	N to S	Features	Facilities	S to N	
N.C. 8	56.7	Winding Stair Gap, U.S. 64; **Franklin, N.C., P.O. 28734** (w on A.T.; P.O.,G,L,M 10m E)	☆ RGLMw	109.8	
	59.8	Wallace Gap, "Old 64" (3,738')	R	106.7	
	60.4	Rock Gap, Standing Indian Campground (C 1.5m W)	RC	106.1	
	60.5	Rock Gap Shelter	Sw	106.0	
	63.0	Glassmine Gap		103.5	
	64.0	Long Branch Shelter	Sw	102.5	
	66.4	Albert Mountain (5,250')		100.1	
N.C. Section 9	66.7	Bearpen Trail, USFS 67	R	99.8	
	67.7	Spring	w	98.8	
	68.0	Mooney Gap, USFS 83	R	98.5	**N.C.–Ga. Map 2**
	68.9	Betty Creek Gap (4,300')	Cw	97.6	
	72.6	Carter Gap Shelter	Sw	93.9	
	73.0	Timber Ridge Trail		93.5	
	75.8	Beech Gap (4,460')	Cw	90.7	
	78.7	Lower Trail Ridge Trail, Standing Indian Mountain (5,498') (w 0.2m W)	w	87.8	
N.C. Section 10	80.2	Standing Indian Shelter	Sw	86.3	
	81.1	Deep Gap, USFS 71 (4,341')	Rw	85.4	
	83.2	Wateroak Gap		83.3	*Nantahala Hiking Club*
	84.1	Chunky Gal Trail		82.4	
	84.3	Whiteoak Stamp	w	82.2	
	85.1	Muskrat Creek Shelter (4,600')	Sw	81.4	
	86.0	Sassafras Gap		80.5	

North Carolina–Georgia

GBS	N to S	Features	Facilities (see page 8 for codes)	S to N	Map
	Miles from Fontana Dam, N.C.		*Miles from Springer Mountain, Ga.*		
	87.9	Bly Gap (3,840')	Cw	78.6	
	88.0	North Carolina–Georgia Line		78.5	
	89.9	Rich Cove Gap		76.6	
	90.1	Campsite	Cw	76.4	
	91.1	Blue Ridge Gap (3,020')		75.4	
	91.7	As Knob		74.8	
	92.4	Plumorchard Gap Shelter (S,w 0.2m E)	Sw	74.1	
	93.6	Bull Gap (3,550')		72.9	
	95.1	Cowart Gap		71.4	
	95.8	Campsite	Cw	70.7	
	96.9	Dicks Creek Gap, U.S. 76 (2,675'); **Hiawassee, Ga., P.O. 30546** (w on A.T.; L 3.5m W; P.O.,G,L,M 11m W)	☆ RGLMw	69.6	
	97.5	Streams	w	69.0	
	98.1	Moreland Gap		68.4	
	99.1	Powell Mountain (3,850')		67.4	
	99.3	McClure Gap	C	67.2	
	100.5	Deep Gap Shelter (3,550') (S,w 0.3m E)	Sw	66.0	
	101.3	Kelly Knob (4,276')		65.2	
	102.3	Addis Gap (3,304') (C,w 0.5m E)	Cw	64.2	
	103.2	Sassafras Gap	w	63.3	
	104.3	Swag of the Blue Ridge		62.2	
	107.9	Tray Mountain Shelter (S 0.2m W; w 0.3m W)	Sw	58.6	
	108.4	Tray Mountain (4,430')		58.1	

Georgia A.T. Club

N.C. Section 11

Ga. Section 12

N.C.–Ga. Map 3

North Carolina–Georgia

GBS	N to S	Features	Facilities (see page 8 for codes)	S to N	Map

Miles from Fontana Dam, N.C.

Miles from Springer Mountain, Ga.

	N to S	Features	Facilities	S to N	
Ga. Section 12	109.2	Tray Gap, Tray Mountain Road (USFS 79/698)	R	57.3	
	109.9	Cheese Factory Site	Cw	56.6	
	110.2	Tray Mountain Road (USFS 79)	R	56.3	
	110.9	Indian Grave Gap, USFS 283 (3,113')	R	55.6	
	112.2	Rocky Mountain (4,017')	C	54.3	
	113.0	Stream	w	53.5	
	113.6	Unicoi Gap, Ga. 75 (2,949'); **Helen, Ga., P.O. 30545** (P.O.,G,L,M 9m E; C,G,L,M 3.8m W)	☆ RCGLM	52.9	
Ga. Section 13	115.1	Blue Mountain (4,025')		51.4	N.C.–Ga. Map 3
	116.0	Blue Mountain Shelter	Sw	50.5	
	116.7	Spring	w	49.8	
	116.9	Campsite	C	49.6	
	117.6	Red Clay Gap		48.9	
	118.3	Chattahoochee Gap (3,500')	w	48.2	
	119.5	Cold Springs Gap		47.0	*Georgia A.T. Club*
	121.9	Poplar Stamp Gap	Cw	44.6	
	123.3	Low Gap Shelter (3,050')	Sw	43.2	
	124.1	Sheep Rock Top		42.4	
	125.9	Poor Mountain		40.6	
	127.0	White Oak Stamp		39.5	
	127.9	Hogpen Gap, Ga. 348 (3,450')	Rw	38.6	
	128.1	Whitley Gap Shelter (S 1.2m E; w 1.5m E)	Sw	38.4	
	128.8	Tesnatee Gap, Ga. 348 (3,138')	R	37.7	
Ga. 14	129.8	Cowrock Mountain (3,842')		36.7	
	130.6	Baggs Creek Gap	Cw	35.9	
	131.1	Wolf Laurel Top		35.4	
	131.8	Rock Spring Top	w	34.7	

North Carolina–Georgia

GBS	N to S	Features	Facilities (see page 8 for codes)	S to N	Map

Miles from Fontana Dam, N.C.   *Miles from Springer Mountain, Ga.*

	N to S	Features	Facilities	S to N	
	132.6	Swaim Gap		33.9	
	133.3	Levelland Mountain (3,942')		33.2	
	133.7	Bull Gap	Cw	32.8	
	134.8	Neel Gap, U.S. 19/129 (3,125')			
		(G,L on A.T.; L 0.3m E;			
		C,G 3m W; C,L 3.5m W)	RCGLw	31.7	
	135.8	Flatrock Gap, Trail to Byron Reece Memorial			
		(w 0.2m W)	w	30.7	
	137.2	Blood Mountain Shelter (4,461')	S(nw)	29.3	
	138.0	Slaughter Creek Campsites	Cw	28.5	
	138.1	Slaughter Creek Trail	w	28.4	
	138.4	Bird Gap (3,650'), Woods Hole Shelter			
		(S,w 0.5m W)	CSw	28.1	
	139.8	Jarrard Gap (3,250')			
		(w 0.3m W; w 1m W, G,L 2m W)	GLw	26.7	
	140.3	Burnett Field Mountain		26.2	
	143.1	Dan Gap		23.4	
	144.4	Big Cedar Mountain (3,737')		22.1	
	145.4	Woody Gap, Ga. 60 (3,173');			
		Suches, Ga., P.O. 30572	☆		
		(w 0.1m W; P.O.,C,G 2m W)	RCGw	21.1	
	146.9	Ramrock Mountain		19.6	
	149.2	Gooch Gap, USFS 42 (2,821')	Rw	17.3	
	150.7	Gooch Mountain Shelter			
		(C,S,w 0.1m W)	CSw	15.8	
	152.2	Justus Creek (2,550')	Cw	14.3	
	153.6	Justus Mountain (3,224')		12.9	
	154.3	Cooper Gap, USFS 42/80	R	12.2	
	156.0	Horse Gap (2,673')	R	10.5	

Georgia A.T. Club

Ga.14 · Ga. Section 15 · Ga. Section 16

N.C.–Ga. Map 4

North Carolina–Georgia

GBS	N to S	Features	Facilities (see page 8 for codes)	S to N	Map
		Miles from Fontana Dam, N.C.	*Miles from Springer Mountain, Ga.*		
	157.9	Hightower Gap, USFS 42/69 (2,854')	R	8.6	
	158.4	Hawk Mountain Shelter (S 0.2m W; w 0.4m W)	Sw	8.1	
	160.3	USFS 251	R	6.2	
	161.3	Side trail to Long Creek Falls, junction with Benton MacKaye and Duncan Ridge trails		5.2	
	162.2	Three Forks, USFS 58 (2,530')	RCw	4.3	
	162.3	Benton MacKaye Trail		4.2	
	162.7	Stover Creek	w	3.8	
	163.7	Stover Creek Shelter (S,w 0.2m E)	Sw	2.8	
	164.6	Benton MacKaye Trail		1.9	
	165.5	USFS 42	R	1.0	
	166.3	Southern terminus, Benton MacKaye Trail; Springer Mountain Shelter (C,S,w 0.2m E)	CSw	0.2	
	166.5	Springer Mountain (3,782')		0.0	

Ga. Section 17

N.C.–Ga. Map 4 · Georgia A.T. Club

Amicalola Falls Approach Trail

GBS	N to S	Features	Facilities (see page 8 for codes)	S to N	Map

Miles from Springer Mountain, Ga.

Miles from Amicalola Falls State Park

	N to S	Features	Facilities	S to N	
	0.0	Springer Mountain (3,782')		8.8	
	1.5	Black Gap Shelter	CSw	7.3	
	2.8	Nimblewill Gap, USFS 28 (3,100')	R	6.0	
	3.4	Side trail to Len Foote Hike Inn (L,M,w 1m E)	LMw	5.4	
	3.7	Frosty Mountain Road (USFS 46)	R	5.1	
	4.0	Frosty Mountain (3,382')	Cw	4.8	
	5.6	High Shoals Road	R	3.2	
	7.3	USFS 46	R	1.5	
	7.4	Side trail to Len Foote Hike Inn (L,M,w 5m E)	LMw	1.4	
	7.6	Amicalola Lodge Road (L,M,w 0.2m E)	RLMw	1.2	
	8.8	Visitors Center, Amicalola Falls State Park (1,700')	RCSw	0.0	

Georgia A.T. Club

Approach Trail

N.C.–Ga. Map 4

A.T. Maintaining Clubs

Maine A.T. Club	www.matc.org
Appalachian Mountain Club	www.outdoors.org
Randolph Mountain Club	www.randolphmountainclub.org
Dartmouth Outing Club	www.dartmouth.edu/~doc
Green Mountain Club	www.greenmountainclub.org
AMC Berkshire Chapter	www.amcberkshire.org
AMC Connecticut Chapter	www.ct-amc.org
New York–New Jersey Trail Conference	www.nynjtc.org
Wilmington Trail Club	www.wilmingtontrailclub.org
Batona Hiking Club	www.batonahikingclub.org
AMC Delaware Valley Chapter	www.amcdv.org
Philadelphia Trail Club	philadelphiatrailclub.org
Blue Mountain Eagle Climbing Club	www.bmecc.org
Allentown Hiking Club	www.allentownhikingclub.org
Susquehanna A.T. Club	www.satc-hike.org
York Hiking Club	www.yorkhikingclub.com
Cumberland Valley A.T. Club	www.cvatclub.org
Mountain Club of Maryland	www.mcomd.org
Potomac A.T. Club	www.patc.net
Old Dominion A.T. Club	www.odatc.net
Tidewater A.T. Club	www.tidewateratc.org
Natural Bridge A.T. Club	www.nbatc.org
Roanoke A.T. Club	www.ratc.org
Outdoor Club of Virginia Tech	www.outdoor.org.vt.edu
Piedmont A.T. Hikers	www.path-at.org
Mount Rogers A.T. Club	www.mratc.org
Tennessee Eastman Hiking Club	www.tehcc.org
Carolina Mountain Club	www.carolinamountainclub.org
Smoky Mountains Hiking Club	www.smhclub.org
Nantahala Hiking Club	www.nantahalahikingclub.org
Georgia A.T. Club	www.georgia-atclub.org

History of the *Appalachian Trail Data Book*

The model for the *Appalachian Trail Data Book* was the "Mileage Fact Sheet" compiled by Ed Garvey and Gus Crews, published simultaneously in 1971 by the Appalachian Trail Conference and Appalachian Books (Oakton, Va.) as an appendix to Mr. Garvey's *Appalachian Hiker*.

The first edition (1977) of the *Appalachian Trail Data Book* was compiled by Raymond F. Hunt of Kingsport, Tenn., who continued to perform this volunteer service annually until 1983, when he began a six-year term as chair of the ATC.

The last 31 editions have been compiled by another volunteer, Daniel D. Chazin of Teaneck, N.J., an officer of the New York–New Jersey Trail Conference and editor of the *Appalachian Trail Guide to New York–New Jersey.* Mr. Chazin draws each fall on the work of field editors of the other 10 guidebooks and more than 30 other volunteer data compilers and Conservancy representatives for information on the various sections of the Appalachian Trail.

The Appalachian Trail Community Network

The Appalachian Trail Community program is an ATC initiative that seeks to develop mutually beneficial relationships with interested towns and counties along the Trail to enhance their economies, further protect the Trail, and engage a new generation of volunteers.

Communities designated as of December 2012 are:

Millinocket, Maine
Monson, Maine
Rangeley, Maine
Hanover, New Hampshire
Norwich, Vermont
Great Barrington, Massachusetts
Dover & Pawling, New York
Warwick, New York
Delaware Water Gap, Pennsylvania
Duncannon, Pennsylvania
Boiling Springs, Pennsylvania
Waynesboro, Pennsylvania
Harpers Ferry/Bolivar, West Virginia
Front Royal/Warren County, Virginia
Luray/Page County, Virginia
Harrisonburg, Virginia
Nelson County, Virginia
Waynesboro, Virginia
Buena Vista, Virginia
Glasgow, Virginia
Troutville, Virginia
Narrows, Virginia
Pearisburg, Virginia
Bland, Virginia
Marion/Smyth County, Virginia
Abingdon, Virginia
Damascus, Virginia

Unicoi County (Erwin), Tennessee
Hot Springs, North Carolina
Franklin, North Carolina
Hiawassee/Towns County, Georgia
Helen/White County, Georgia
Union County (Blairsville, Suches), Georgia
Dahlonega, Georgia
Ellijay/Gilmer County, Georgia

Those listed in the *Data Book* are indicated by a ☆ in the Facilities column.

**Protect, enhance, and promote
the Trail experience:
That's what we do.**

You can help
by joining the
Appalachian Trail Conservancy
today!

You can become a member
by going to
www.appalachiantrail.org/join
or calling
(304) 535-6331